LA
BELLA VITA

LA
BELLA VITA

*Live and Love
the Italian Way*

AMINDA LEIGH & PIETRO PESCE

Avon, Massachusetts

*For my adored father, Gordon Leigh,
whose passion for words was such an inspiration.*

Published by
Adams Media, a division of F+W Media, Inc.
57 Littlefield Street, Avon, MA 02322. U.S.A.
www.adamsmedia.com

ISBN 10: 1-59869-902-4
ISBN 13: 978-1-59869-902-9
eISBN 10: 1-4405-0906-9
eISBN 13: 978-1-4405-0906-3

Printed in the United States of America.

10 9 8 7 6 5 4 3 2 1

Library of Congress Cataloging-in-Publication Data
is available from the publisher.

This publication is designed to provide accurate and authoritative information with regard
to the subject matter covered. It is sold with the understanding that the publisher is not en-
gaged in rendering legal, accounting, or other professional advice. If legal advice or other expert assistance is required, the services of a competent professional person should be sought.
—From a *Declaration of Principles* jointly adopted by a Committee of the American Bar
Association and a Committee of Publishers and Associations

Many of the designations used by manufacturers and sellers to distinguish their product are
claimed as trademarks. Where those designations appear in this book and Adams Media was
aware of a trademark claim, the designations have been printed with initial capital letters.

*This book is available at quantity discounts for bulk purchases.
For information, please call 1-800-289-0963.*

CONTENTS

ACKNOWLEDGMENTS

First and foremost, we must give our heartfelt thanks to our agent, Lisa DiMona, who has guided us with clarity and insight throughout the writing of this book. We look forward to welcoming you to Italy to show you its delights first hand instead of describing them to you over the phone. We also want to express our appreciation for the work done by Paula Munier, Laura Daly, and the publishing team at Adams Media for putting their faith in us. The next special thanks goes to our parents, Sylvia and the late Gordon Leigh, and Erminia and Olivierio Pesce. We are extremely grateful for all their copious support, whether physical, mental, moral, or emotional. We could not have done it without them. We also thank all those family members, friends, and colleagues who have accompanied us through this tour of the six senses of Italian life, with a special thanks going to our cherished, now departed Checca and all the Thursday night dinner crew (*gruppo della cena del giovedì*). Everyone has generously contributed their anecdotes and ideas, offered endless backup, support, hot dinners, and the occasional glass of wine—just like a true Italian circle of loved ones.

We would also like to specifically mention the following people for their precious input and inspiration, listed in strictly alphabetical order: Giordano Angeletti, Ferdinando Beltrano, Andrea Bevilacqua, Alessandro Borghese, Barbara Bouchet, Karina Bouchet, Dave

Caplan, Trish Carlson, Jenna Charlebois, Cinque, Suzanne Curletto, MC, Maria Delourdes Lopez, Jim Dessicino, Darcy DiMona, Fibi Duke, Jessica Edwards, Eleonora, Elvira, Alessandra Guidoni, Alex Karshan, Sylvia Leigh, Gordon Leigh, Sydney Leigh, Lisa and Juno, Stuart Mabey, Tiffany McIver, Alex Nartowicz, Michelle Noon, Francesca Palombelli, Annamaria Pasetti, the wider Pesce family: Giovanni and Natalia, Lorenzo and Giulia, Laura plus teenagers Lorenzo (Jr.) and Jacopo, Pivio, Gauri Sathe, Silvio Scotti, Lisa Shanley, CS, Chris and Victoria Springall, RS, Rick Thompson, Alison Victoria, Jami West, and Sophie West. If we have missed anyone, please forgive us; your contribution was greatly appreciated nonetheless.

IN LOVE WITH ITALY

Innamorata dell'Italia

Italians have often been described as true hedonists, and with good reason—they devote themselves to savoring all the pleasures and beauty life can offer, from food to fashion, sensuality to style, language to nature. And they do so in breathtaking surroundings, enjoying life to the fullest, with a passion unique to Italians. They eat with passion, they socialize with passion, they speak with passion, and, of course, they love with passion! In Italy, it doesn't matter if you're poor or you're not well educated or you live on the wrong side of the tracks—you still turn heads if you know how to flash a winning smile, cast a sultry glance, sway your hips in a sexy way, engage in witty repartee, dress with style or flair, and, above all, exude the sense that you are your own person and know your own worth.

But what is so special about the Italian way of living that makes it worth passing on? Well, adopting the Italian approach to life, enjoying the here and now and reveling in the pleasures to be found even in the most simple of pastimes, can potentially make you happier! And who doesn't want to be happier? Adopting the Italians' laid-back approach can encourage you to relax and devote more time to doing things you enjoy; emulating their eye for fashion means you can improve your style and increase your self-confidence; and cooking like an Italian means you will eat better and savor your food much more—without having to spend a fortune.

Last, but not least, loving like an Italian can raise your erotic passion to new heights. Just take a look at the way the current Italian Prime Minister, Silvio Berlusconi, behaves—flirting with young women and showering them with compliments. An eternal optimist, he's never deterred by the fact that he's in his seventies (or the fact that he has been married—though his second wife filed for divorce proceedings as news stories about his alleged dalliances profilerated). Age knows no barriers in Italy: you can be a prime contender as a *gentiluomo* (gentlemen), *galante* (chivalrous) and *passionale* (passionate), until your dying day. Naturally, the same applies to women too.

When American actor George Clooney was asked by a journalist at the Venice Film Festival why he had moved to Italy (he lives for a large part of the year in a *villa* on the shores of Lake Como), he recounted the following story as an explanation: "I was walking through the village at sunset one day and I saw a builder, still covered in plaster and wearing his overalls, carrying *una bottiglia di vino* (a bottle of wine) and a bunch of flowers. He was obviously going home to his woman and was taking her a small token of his affection. You would never see that in America!"

Since Italians devote their time to making the most of each sense to make their lives richer and better, this guide is organized into chapters covering each of the five senses: *vista* (sight), *udito* (hearing), *tatto* (touch), *olfatto* (smell), and *gusto* (taste). However, even all five senses don't fully encompass the fundamental facets of Italian life and love, so you'll find an additional "sixth sense," dubbed *la bella vita* (the beautiful life). Within each chapter are sections touching on separate themes in the Italian attitude to loving and living, giving you *l'Italia in tutti sensi* (Italy, in all senses).

Every chapter is loaded with pointers on how to excite, enhance, or stimulate each particular sense, thus creating the beautiful life typical of a passionate Italian. You'll also find tips on language, style, cooking, and flirting that you can practice at home, as well as the lowdown on what awaits you should you decide to take the plunge and experience Italian life first-hand.

The ancient Roman dramatist and philosopher Lucius Annaeus Seneca famously said "*La felicità è un bene vicinissimo, alla portata di tutti: basta fermarsi e raccoglierla*" (happiness is a gift that is very close at hand to everyone: you just need to stop and grab it), and this guide is designed to help you do just that, in true Italian style.

ONE

LOVE AT FIRST SIGHT

amore a prima vista

Italy: the home of sumptuous art, gorgeous surroundings, and stylish dressers. The Italians' sense of *vista* (sight) is undoubtedly innundated with beauty all day, every day. This is a country with more than 2,000 years of practice in the art of creating and appreciating the finer things in life. Admiring *bellezza* (beauty) in all its forms—whether the human body, the natural world, or manmade objects—is so deeply engrained in Italians' everyday life that putting on a show is almost second nature to them.

DID YOU KNOW ?

The city of Milan is considered by many to be the world's fashion capital for both men and women because of the marriage of luxury ready-to-wear collections and input from top-name designers, many based in the city. Milan is one of the four locations to host the major, high-profile fashion weeks (New York starts the season, followed by London, then Milan, and finally Paris)—a must-see event for any fashionista.

This chapter shows how developing an appreciation for beauty can enhance your life and relationships, whether it's sprucing up your wardrobe, engaging in flirtatious eye contact, or taking inspiration from the stars of Italy's silver screen.

CUTTING A DASH

Renowned the world over for their beauty, Italian women are admired for their voluptuous curves; large, flashing eyes; and long, silken locks. And Italy's men are a pretty good match, with their chiseled features, sultry looks, and dazzling smiles. One of the primary national "sports" in Italy is *vedere e farsi vedere* (to see and be seen). Most of Italian society revolves around this activity in one way or another. For example, the Italians' famous love for the *passeggiata* (stroll) is so widespread because people get to strut their stuff and watch other people strut theirs.

Closely linked to this mania of being seen is the importance placed on the *bella figura*. In Italy, you will hear this phrase used in many different contexts with slightly varied meanings, but here it signifies cutting a "fine figure," or looking good (*bella figura* can also mean making the right impression or acting appropriately). Italians consider the opposite, a *brutta figura* (unkempt figure) to be highly shameful and embarrassing, and people will go to any length to avoid making this impression. This social pressure means Italians are expected to take pride in their looks, which should be *in stagione* (fashionable and up-to-date) and *curato* (carefully assembled), whatever the time of day and wherever you are going.

In any location where Italians gather, you will see them eyeing each other. Women look at other women and even men check each other out. They take in the overall picture, then verify the small details, such as the haircut, the nail polish color, or the brand of purse.

Italian television also reflects this habit of looking each other up and down: TV camera shots sweep lingeringly upward from a person's feet—particularly if it's a woman—past her legs, slowing down over her torso to finally come to a stop on a close-up of her face. While general social pressure inevitably plays its part, the overriding factor in looking good for Italians is a genuine pride in their appearance. They always want to look their best and are happy to put in the effort to make sure they do.

LIVE *LA BELLA VITA*
Don't Give Up!

Some Americans begin to pay less attention to their appearance once they are in a serious relationship or as they get older. In Italy, that's never the case! All Italian women—mothers, the elderly, wives—have their hair cut and colored, put on lipstick (*rossetto*) and makeup, use nail polish (*smalto*), wear heels, and sport low-cut tops. Even if you're eighty, this attire is not considered inappropriate in Italy, as long as it is worn with style, attitude, and confidence. It is also fairly common to see women wearing bikinis, even if they are over fifty or pregnant, whereas in many other countries the subliminal message for women over a certain age is, "You're too old (or large) for a bikini and must wear a one-piece bathing suit."

A friend told us a story that perfectly sums up the Italians' priorities. She was learning to drive and came to a rotary where she had to stop for oncoming traffic. As she was waiting for a gap, the instructor said to her, "So, in Italy, who has right of way at a rotary?" She thought she had this one nailed and smugly replied, "People coming from left, because Italians drive on the right." The driving instructor shook his head woefully and said, "No, no. *Una bella donna* [a beautiful woman] always has right of way at a rotary!"

AGE DOESN'T MATTER

This pursuit of beauty and *bella figura* is not only a pastime of the young. In Italy, you see many middle-aged or older people who *si curano* (take care of their appearance), undaunted by their age, strutting their style proudly. Ask yourself if you do this too, or if you've "given up" to some degree. Though you want to dress in an age-appropriate way, you can still put on a show no matter how old you are. Italians could not be accused of being ageist—their elderly population is still active in virtually all areas of society, and generally they don't "let themselves go." A prime example is national icon Sophia Loren, who appeared as a seminude pinup for the famous Pirelli calendar at the age of seventy-two!

BECOME "EYE CANDY"

Glamorous, elegant, stylish, impeccable, and attractive: the list of adjectives describing the Italians' appearance is endless. How do they pull off being so (apparently) effortlessly chic and beautiful? Well, the first myth to quash is that this look is totally carefree; Italians go to great lengths to make sure they're well groomed—it's just that the *fatica* (effort) usually goes on behind the scenes. Unlike people in many other nations, who choose clothing and shoes predominantly for their functionality rather than their beauty, Italians prefer to turn their bodies into "eye candy" for all to admire. Why? It shows that they care about their appearance and that they want to present themselves in a way that reflects their personality, their tastes, and their style. The next time you think about throwing on a pair of sweats, ask yourself: Does this outfit make me feel beautiful? Smart? Self-confident? Is this the image of me I want the world to see? Whether going to an opera or the market, Italians strive to project the best image of themselves. How can you do the same thing in your own life? We'll talk about specific fashion tips shortly, but first, here are a few general ideas to consider.

Ask Your Partner for Help

Knowing which clothing best suits your figure is quite an art. But here's a tip you can pick up from Italians: Let your partner help you. Believe it or not, partners can really lend a hand with this, acting as a true, honest, and loving mirror to reflect how you appear to the outside world. Italian men are particularly skilled at appraising their lover's appearance, because they follow fashion trends and have an expert eye for beauty. They adore their lover's body for what it is, though they're not afraid to tell her if she needs to lose a few pounds, and may even give her tips on how to elegantly disguise that fact in the meantime! Even if your man isn't as fashion conscious as an Italian man, he can still tell you what he thinks you look best in and why. If you're not in a relationship right now, ask a trusted friend to give you an honest opinion.

Pietro Says

When you see a pretty woman who is well put together and walks with confidence, *ti tira su* (she gives you a lift—yes, in all senses of the word!). After all, it's a pleasure to look at someone who takes care of herself. Yes, you can criticize Italians for being too materialistic and obsessed with designer clothes, but try taking a page out of their book on the grooming front and make more of an effort when going out in public. It needn't take much and can boost your self-confidence knowing you're looking good.

In a world where women are justifiably campaigning for equal rights, asking for and taking advice from your lover about your appearance may seem like a step backward in time. But if the question is asked and answered with love, the result shouldn't be condescending or chauvinistic, but rather, genuine and heartfelt. You may even find the increased level of intimacy can supercharge your romance. Ask your partner to be honest instead of just throwing a passing glance and saying "You look great, honey!" Honesty can help you improve your appearance—and if your partner can't tell you how you really look, who can?

Splurge on Quality

Fads come and go, but certain general characteristics remain in the Italians' style of dressing. They are willing to spend money on well-tailored clothes, made of good quality fabrics that don't easily pill or fray. So before you grab three cheap shirts on sale for a total of $25, ask yourself if your money would be better spent on one high-quality $25 shirt.

LIVE *LA BELLA VITA*
When to Visit Italy

Remember, Italy can get very hot from June to August (with peaks of more than 100°F), making it pretty exhausting and uncomfortable when you are trying to see all the sights along with the other sweaty tourists bravely sweltering in the heat. Many Italians "escape the city" in the summer, so some shops and restaurants may be closed *per ferie* (for vacation). Spring and autumn are welcoming seasons, and if you like fireworks, New Year's is a great time to visit. Italians love *fuochi d'artificio*, and everyone puts on pyrotechnic displays to herald the New Year, even launching them from their own terraces and balconies.

YOUR *PARADISO*

MUSIC BY MOONLIGHT

Apart from the many music festivals held in Italy (perhaps the most famous being the Sanremo Music Festival of Italian Song), in the summer virtually the whole country takes advantage of the good weather to turn the streets into one enormous open-air venue for concerts of all kinds. You can catch live music on stages erected on museum steps, in Roman ruins, beautiful gardens, the local piazza, ancient amphitheatres, and green parks. Most towns and cities hold summer seasons of live events, with food kiosks, bars, markets, and seating areas set up for the occasion, making concert going a total-sensorial experience. If you're headed to Italy, check the local tourist office to see what concerts are available in the area you're visiting.

Don't Follow the Crowd

It's also worth noting that Italy's rich tend to hide the fact they're rich—they dress smartly but avoid any overly ostentatious show of wealth. If you look closely, you will see that the sweater casually tied around his shoulders is pure cashmere or that the purse swinging from her wrist is by a top designer, but you have to look for these things, as they are not brazenly flashed about. Brand names *are* important to the Italians (as we'll discuss next), but more for the quality and the social cache they represent than for the amount of money they cost.

DID YOU KNOW ?

For *Capodanno* (New Year's), it is traditional for highly superstitious Italians to wear red underwear, which they believe brings good luck. This applies not just to women but also to men and kids. In December, lingerie boutiques in Italy are crammed with all kinds of red underwear for him and her. Even though many people already have lots of red undies at home, the idea is to wear a new pair (bought for you by someone else) to usher in the new year.

ITALIANS AND THEIR DESIGNER CLOTHES

Italians are addicted to their designer labels. They consider their branded clothing to be a badge of pride, and indeed the "Made in Italy" trademark is synonymous with top quality fashion throughout the world. After all, how many other countries can boast police officers dressed in uniforms by Armani and national soccer teams wearing specially designed Dolce & Gabbana gear off the field? Italians are willing to fork out large wads of cash for their designer duds, and, if things are financially tough, they are even willing to buy a fake version of their beloved brand just to "keep up with the Joneses" and make sure they look like they can afford to be in fashion. (Recently, however, authorities have clamped down on counterfeited designer items because of copyright breaches and subsequent loss of profit for legitimate operators.)

Top-of-the-Line Italian Designers

Even the most threadbare list of top Italian fashion designers would read like a veritable who's who of the international fashion parade: Armani, Dolce & Gabbana, Gucci, Prada, and Valentino are just a few. They are all established giants; their garments dominate the international runways and are worn the world over. For those not well versed in the realm of Italian fashion designers, here is a basic guide to their style and which celebrities they dress.

ITALIAN DESIGNERS

- **Giorgio Armani:** Worldwide institution, Hollywood darling, and multimillionaire with a fashion career spanning more than three decades. He first won a dedicated following with his signature unstructured jackets and both sexes adore him for his clean-cut tailoring. As worn by: Christian Bale, Cate Blanchett, George Clooney, Matt Damon, Jodie Foster, and Michelle Pfeiffer.

- **Roberto Cavalli:** Known for his extravagant, over-the-top styles embellished with exotic printing techniques, leather and feathers, and oozing with sex appeal and glam rock. As worn by: Halle Berry, Jon Bon Jovi, Bono, Geri Halliwell, Lenny Kravitz,

Alicia Keyes, Beyoncé Knowles, Lindsay Lohan, and Jennifer Lopez.

- **Dolce & Gabbana** (Domenico Dolce and Stefano Gabbana): Exquisite tailoring mixed with stylistic splashes with a particular nod to the style of Italian film legends, has made this fashion house a global brand leader. As worn by: Monica Bellucci, Robert Downey Jr., Joseph Fiennes, Angelina Jolie, Madonna, Kylie Minogue, and Isabella Rossellini.

- **Fendi:** First specializing in furs and handbags, this brand has now expanded into such areas as menswear and sunglasses. Karl Lagerfeld contributes to the range as chief designer. As worn by: Jessica Alba, Eva Mendes, Sarah Jessica Parker, and Charlize Theron.

- **Salvatore Ferragamo:** Though best known for impeccable handmade shoes, this retailer also sells leather goods and ready-to-wear lines for men. As worn by: 2008 Republican presidential candidate John McCain (who kicked up a stir on the campaign trail when spotted wearing a pair of Ferragamo Pregiato Moccasins, which cost more than $500).

- **Gucci:** The iconic Gucci logo graces status symbol accessories and womenswear collections. As worn by: virtually every A-list celebrity, from Jackie Kennedy to Princess Diana, Sophia Loren to Madonna, and John Wayne to Jack Nicholson.

- **Missoni:** Offers luxury knitwear made using traditional Italian handicraft techniques, organic materials, and bright colors. As worn by: Cameron Diaz, Demi Moore, and Sharon Stone.

- **Moschino:** Fuses bold designs together with a dash of wit and whimsy to create fashion with an unusual twist. As worn by: Anna Friel, Gwyneth Paltrow, and Zara Phillips (granddaughter of Queen Elizabeth II).

- **La Perla:** Coveted for sumptuous corsetry and beachwear this designer creates lingerie and underwear collections to die for using an expert knowledge of the female form. It also now offers a line of accessories. As worn by: Anjelica Houston and Daniel Craig (while playing 007 James Bond in the 2006 movie *Casino Royale*).

- **Prada:** Literally fought over in stores, this superbrand expanded from bags and shoes to include mens- and womenswear collections. As worn by: Cameron Diaz, Maggie Gyllenhaal, Salma Hayek, and "the Devil," of course!

- **Valentino (Valentino Garavani):** Fashion idol revered by divas for more than four decades for his extravagant, flawlessly cut evening dresses known for their feminine lines and dramatic embellishments. As worn by: Jennifer Aniston, Joan Collins, Penelope Cruz, and Naomi Watts.

- **Bottega Veneta:** This designer specializes in fine leather goods, in particular super-soft handmade bags. As worn by: Jessica Alba, Katie Holmes, Scarlett Johansson, Nicole Kidman, and Sarah Jessica Parker.

- **Versace:** Adored for its use of bold colors and figure-hugging designs topped off with plenty of glamour, this line is now run by Donatella Versace, who took over after her brother Gianni was killed in 1996. She stated that her 2009 spring/summer menswear collection was inspired by newly elected American president Barack Obama, with clothes for "a relaxed man who doesn't need to flex muscles to show he has power." As worn by: Halle Berry, Jamie Foxx, Elizabeth Hurley, Angelina Jolie, Madonna, Brad Pitt, and Catherine Zeta-Jones.

- **Ermenegildo Zegna:** This brand is most famous for suits, but also offers shirts, ties, coats, and a whole range of men's accessories. Suits can be purchased either ready-to-wear or in the more expensive made-to-measure alternative. As worn by: Javier Bardem and Adrien Brody.

How to Find Top-Notch Italian Designer Clothes at a Discount

You may not be able to afford deluxe designer clothes at full price, but here are some tips for getting them at discounted rates:

- Watch for sales and discounts at the designer's stores or websites, especially around Fashion Week, when you may find more promotions.

- See if the designer offers a more affordable collection within their brand. For example, D&G labels cost less than full-blown

Dolce & Gabbana items; Emporio Armani offers a more accessible sample of designer duds than Armani does; Moschino's Cheap & Chic line is actually more medium priced than really cheap, while the Love Moschino collection is more wallet friendly; and Miu Miu is Prada's answer to budget concerns.

- Find vintage, second-hand designer clothes to save money, look good, and live a sustainable, eco-friendly recycling lifestyle.
- Look online. The Internet has certainly made designer fashion more accessible to the masses thanks to online auctions.
- Visit outlet stores or factory shops that are selling off last season's lines at heavily reduced prices.

LIVE *LA BELLA VITA*
Clothes Need Care Too!

If you do spend serious money on top quality clothing, you should take good care of your investment. Italians would never be seen out in public in a garment that needs cleaning, ironing, or mending. Get into the Italian habit of caring for your clothes by always hanging them up, and ensuring they are clean and impeccably presentable before you don them to go out.

More Affordable Italian Designers

If the previous list of designers seems beyond your financial reach even on sale, there are plenty of other, more affordable Italian brands on the international fashion scene to help you recreate that attractive Italian-style appearance:

- For more luxury women's clothes, particularly dresses and coats that are classic foundation wardrobe pieces transcending the latest fashion trends, try **Max Mara** (or its even more affordable youth offshoot, **Max & Co.**).
- If you're looking for an elegant yet slightly more informal look, check out **Blumarine**.
- If you want to look casual, you can do no better than popping into a branch of the Italian brand leader **Benetton**.
- For stylish jeans and casual wear, try **Diesel**.
- For something quirky and original, try **Fiorucci**, famous for being fun and anti-fashion.
- If you want to hit the gym with a touch of Italian style, look for **Elisabetta Rogiani**, who's been making waves stateside with her sexy activewear that doubles as hip streetwear, worn by celebs like Pamela Anderson, Cameron Diaz, and Lucy Liu.

A LOW-COST WAY TO LOOK ITALIAN: USE COLOR APPROPRIATELY

Designers aside, you don't have to shell out a fortune to add some Italian style to your wardrobe. How? Adopt the creative way Italians use color and tone, and add a pop of bright, eye-catching shades to a plain outfit. The trick is to choose complementary tones that blend well together. For example, lime green and pink can look stunning, as can electric blue and orange. The trick is not to overdo it. Use one central color and then make a splash effect with another contrasting shade using accessories. Even jeans can look stylish if you choose a tailored pair that fit snugly, perhaps with a glitter design on the back pockets, combined with a simple, well cut pressed white shirt and a pair of brightly colored suede boots.

You can reduce the risk of creating an overly garish effect by accompanying a bright color with black or white. Don't wear too many overpatterned items at once, no matter what color they are, as they can be too busy. If bright color is not your thing, you can opt for neutral shades. Try teaming stone with white, and top the look off with a straw bag to add additional texture.

FIND CLOTHES THAT ACTUALLY FIT

Women's tops tend to be much more tightly fitted in Italy than in the States, and shirts are deliberately unbuttoned to almost indecent levels to emphasize cleavage. You probably don't want to go *that* far with your everyday look, however! The point is that clothes should *fit* you, and not be either ridiculously baggy or cutting off your circulation.

Try cleaning up your appearance by following these Italian-style dos and don'ts:

DON'T	DO
Wear hoodies	*Wear tailored, well-cut sweaters or cardigans*
Wear sloppy sweats	*Wear a tailored pair of jeans and a fitted t-shirt*
Wear large, boxy, shapeless boots or shoes	*Wear pumps or boots with a small heel*
Wear white sneakers or tennis shoes (unless you're at the gym or playing tennis)	*Wear comfortable, stylish loafers*
Wear flip flops around town (they're for the beach)	*Wear strappy sandals with a small heel*
Wear mini-shorts	*Wear well-cut, just-above-the-knee shorts or capri pants*
Wear overly patterned, baggy cutoff pants	*Wear fitted pants in one color or with a simple, subtle design*

FOCUS ON FOOTWEAR

For shoe lovers, Italy is a glimpse of heaven. Italians adore their *scarpe* (shoes) and make sure they have at least one pair in the very latest fashion. Italian footwear is distinguished for its wonderful style, highest levels of quality craftsmanship, softest leather, and innovative design. Many people come to Italy just for the shoes, leaving room in their suitcases so they can take home a couple of pairs of the latest models.

Women's High Heels

High heels (*tacchi alti*) dominate the women's market and are certainly not known for comfort. Italian women aren't just wearing their killer heels for the men; they're wearing them for "society." It's all about style and creating a feminine silhouette to knock everyone dead. Practicality does not come into play at all. Italian women know full well that high heels arch the feet and elongate the legs to create a svelte shape, even when they're not at their slimmest. Heels are synonymous with sex appeal the world over because they exude an aura of power, sending subliminal messages that can trigger desire. Italian designers exploit the eroticism of high heels by emphasizing the elegant shape and sexy curve of the shoe.

One of the modern wonders of the world is watching Italian women serenely glide over the treacherous, ankle-breaking cobblestones in four-inch heels as though it were the smoothest sidewalk on earth. These women don't even look down at the ground while they walk, never even seeming to be on the alert for cracks and crevices. How can you achieve that practically Olympic feat? It comes with years of practice and requires a true dedication to beauty over comfort.

Boots

Leather boots (*stivali*) come in all shapes and sizes, and are another staple in the Italian closet. Italian boots often make a dramatic statement, with brightly colored, butter-soft leather, buckles and laces, unusual prints, or eye-catching details. It all depends on that season's fashion. Boots are now being worn all year round, even in the summer. Hot-weather versions tend to be no higher than calf-length, in lighter-colored, softer suede, often punched through with prettily patterned (and highly strategic) holes.

LIVE *LA BELLA VITA*
Take Care of Your Shoes!

Italians are careful to make sure their footwear is fit to be seen in public. Follow their example by always ensuring your shoes and boots are unscuffed and well polished. Also, keep up your footwear maintenance with regular heeling and soling. Don't wait until your shoes are so far worn at the heel that they're beyond repair.

ACCENT WITH ACCESSORIES

Finishing off an outfit with a designer purse, some striking—perhaps even fishnet—hose, an exotic scarf, classic jewelry, and the ubiquitous pair of sunglasses is a given for Italian women, who consider themselves virtually naked without these fundamental accessories. The trick is to carefully choose the colors of these items to match or create a contrast with the rest of your outfit. Even combining different shades with similar tones can look great (for example khaki, yellow, orange, and brown).

DID YOU KNOW ?

The Italian fashion industry is one of the country's most important manufacturing sectors and one of the jewels in the crown of the "Made in Italy" brand. Figures from Italian Fashion System reveal that in 2007, the textile-fashion industry's total sales were worth over 54 billion euros (roughly $80 billion). Italy is ranked highly in the top five of world exports for wool yarns, hosiery, knitwear, and clothing. Above all, Italian fashion is revered for its excellent craftsmanship, exquisite finishing, highest quality textiles, and softest, most supple leather goods.

Sunglasses

One item no Italian would be seen without is a pair of sunglasses (*occhiali da sole*) clamped over their eyes, a year-round essential. Many people sport the latest designer brands, whether huge, jewel-encrusted models or narrow, wire-framed or frameless numbers with colored lenses. If you are going to invest serious bucks on a pair of designer sunglasses, go for a more classic style that can be worn anywhere—to the office, on the beach, or at a funeral. You can then buy some cheaper, more trendy or fun specs as an extra.

There is also a very Italian way to wear your sunglasses when they're not over your eyes. Italian women never shove their glasses upwards into their hair. They make the effort to take off their glasses completely, and then carefully place them neatly in their hair so it doesn't get mussed.

LIVE *LA BELLA VITA*
The Classics Are Always in Style

In order to dress like an Italian, invest the largest proportion of your hard-earned cash on top-quality, classic items, such as suits or dresses. Look for simple, well-cut lines in muted colors, such as black, gray, navy, or brown. You can wear these items time and again while keeping your look fresh and fashionable by mixing cheaper, more trendy pieces with the rest of your wardrobe. Ensure clothes are well cut and tailored, and if they don't fit you quite right when you buy them off the shelf, go to a tailor for alterations. For example, pulling up a dress strap by half an inch can boost your cleavage—it will be money well spent.

Beach Accessories

If you are going to the beach, choose a colored pareo or towel to set off your bikini in true Italian style. It may seem paradoxical, but Italian women actually tend to cover up more than you may expect in the summertime. They use flimsy shawls or large scarves in semi-transparent material to hint at the body underneath. This is much more sexy and alluring than flaunting acres of bare flesh. If your underwear must be seen, make sure it's not a graying bra strap but a sexy number that suggests you are wearing something beautiful and tempting underneath. You can also buy bras with transparent straps, which have become popular to pair with flimsy summer dresses and skimpy vests.

Sparkle

Italian women always have a touch of sparkle somewhere—on jeans, shoes, purses, or even in makeup—which catches the light and creates *allegria* (gaiety). Even female TV news anchors wear brightly colored, low-cut shirts and large sparkly, dangly earrings verging on tacky. Beware: bright colors and a splash of sparkle look great in the Mediterranean light, but may not fit so well in a climate with more gray skies and less sun—unless you really want to stand out!

If you want to add some strategically placed sparkle to your look, don't go over the top—you don't want to end up looking gaudy and cheap. Try some judicious amounts of the following (and not all together!):

- Sequins
- Glitter

- Sparkly makeup—around eyes, on top of cheekbones, or even around your cleavage for evenings out
- Shimmery handbag
- Shiny belt (or a belt with a shiny buckle)
- One large piece of glittery jewelry (choose a necklace, ring, OR bracelet)

GROUNDING IN GROOMING

To properly imitate Italian style, you need to pay attention to your overall grooming. Some tips for women:

- A little makeup is a must before leaving the house (perhaps just a touch of mascara and lipstick), even if you're only going to the store. An Italian man would highly disapprove if his partner were to go out in public without any makeup.
- An Italian woman will always make sure her hair is regularly cut (and often colored; you won't catch many Italian women sporting graying "badger roots"), and she combs her tresses to a silken sheen, using a small mirror to check the back of her hair in a larger mirror.
- Keep your nail polish fresh and make sure it's not cracked, fading, or streaky. Both your fingernails and your toenails should look as though they were professionally done that morning.

If you're in a relationship with an Italian man, he will expect you to always make an effort and look good in public; he will probably even chastise you if you don't. However, they abide by the same high standards!

FASHION IS FOR MEN, TOO

It's obvious that if Italian men expect their partners to look elegant and put together when going out, they can hardly walk around looking untidy or unfashionable themselves; the comparison would be far too humiliating. You will never (well, hardly ever) see Italian men wearing sneakers and baseball caps with shapeless cutoff pants and grubby, sweat-stained t-shirts. If they dared to be seen out in public like that, they'd attract a lot of attention, but not for the right reasons.

What Men Should Wear

Help your partner dress the Italian way by adopting these fashion philosophies:

- When the occasion calls for a suit, Italian men choose muted colors like navy and charcoal in soft wool or wool-blend fabrics for the winter. To make more of a statement, they team these somber suits up with lighter, sometimes even pastel, shirts (in shades from muted purple to vibrant blue or pale orange), and add a final splash with dazzling ties.
- In warm weather, men should wear suits made of best quality linen or fine cotton, in pale neutral shades like cream or stone.

- For a more informal look, men can wear a pair of well-cut chinos or some "urban chic" jeans, worn with a polo shirt in a contrasting color (even a pastel shade) and a loosely tailored jacket—either in leather, linen, cotton, or wool, depending on the season.

- Naturally, Italian men also wear the best shoes. You will never catch them wearing anything other than a pair of stylish brogues, elegant lace-ups, or boots. Footwear is important to create the right image of the suave man about town with a beautiful woman at his side. It just doesn't work when he's sporting a dirty pair of sneakers or a scuffed pair of worn-at-the-heel shoes. Whatever shoes your man chooses, they should always be well-polished, properly heeled, and soled. Italian men even manage to look elegant wearing sandals in the summertime, and you will *never* catch them wearing socks underneath. There are lighter shoes made with softer leather that can be cool yet elegant when the heat is on.

Men's Accessories

Just like Italian women, Italian men pay careful attention to detail, especially with accessories. Try these ideas to keep your accessories in line with Italian style:

- Don't insist on wearing your same old favorite ties, time-and-again. Fashions change and Italian designers certainly offer lines packed with the latest trends in color, size, and cut. Also keep an eye out to see what tie knots are *alla moda* (fashionable).

- An Italian leather belt with an eye-catching buckle can really complete a look.
- Italian men do not shy from wearing jewelry, though they are more likely to go for a single "statement piece" like a bracelet, classic ring, or a neck chain with a chunky pendant. His jewelry should blend in with the rest of his overall appearance.

CULTIVATE CONFIDENCE

One thing Italian men and women are not lacking in is self-confidence—it simply oozes from every pore. Even not-so-attractive Italians hold themselves with an assurance, an attitude, and a confidence that almost automatically make them appear attractive. They clearly feel comfortable and natural in their own skin. This is a quality unique to Italians—elsewhere in the world, you often see beautiful people looking like a sack of potatoes because they carry themselves poorly or are evidently full of insecurities.

One way to instantly convey this self-confidence is by changing the way you walk. Add a subtle sway to your hips (*sculettare*)—nothing more than a slight wiggle radiates sexiness—don't go too overboard with the swagger though: you don't want to seem arrogant or unapproachable. This goes for both men and women. Remember to always walk straight with your shoulders back and your head held high to further enhance your aura of self-confidence. You will also ruin your sex goddess image if you are rushing about looking flustered or hassled. The idea is to walk slowly but with purpose, you want to give people time to appreciate your beauty and the effort you've made with your outfit and grooming.

LIVE *LA BELLA VITA*
Buy Your Partner Italian Men's Jewelry

One of the popular gifts the superstitious Italians like giving is the *corno* or the Devil's horn amulet. These obviously come in the shape of a horn, and can range from simple red necklace pendants or fancy versions in coral, gold, or silver. The corno is mainly worn by men as it is believed to ward off curses on their manliness; however, it is also worn by women as a charm against the *malocchio* (evil eye).

UNDERSTANDING ITALIAN EYE CONTACT

One fundamental part of Italian social interaction is eye contact. A passing glance across a crowded bar or *piazza*, or even exchanged in line at a store can provide a *brivido di piacere* (shiver of pleasure). Eye contact is much more intense in Italy than, say, in the States; the men in Italy will lock you into their gaze. This heavy-duty eye contact continues throughout courtship and beyond.

Eye Contact with Strangers

When dealing with people they don't know, non-Italians tend to avoid direct eye contact completely or keep it to a minimum because it could have unpredictable and sometimes even dangerous consequences. But in Italy, swapping flirty glances is an everyday passion among *sconosciuti* (strangers). These fleeting visual encounters of the erotic kind usually just end there, but they bear the delicious, hidden promise of what might have been.

Pietro Says

I have an American friend who noticed a big difference in how beauty is perceived in Italy and the States. He's come across many stunningly beautiful American women with long legs and sculpted bodies, but each one is teeming with neurotic complexes. In Italy, even if a woman has legs like tree stumps, she thinks she's the cat's meow and presents herself as such, which he found very sexy. Women in Italy just exude a highly contagious attitude of "I'm beautiful."

In some respects flirting could even be considered compulsory in Italy; you're considered strange if you *don't* do it. Sometimes it goes beyond just eye contact and is followed up with a compliment and then a flirty chat. This happens among all age groups and across generations. Older Italian men still think they're in the running; they don't consider a discrepancy in age as a barrier to flirting. To some ears, this may seem inappropriate or even bordering on sleazy, but in Italy it's all just an innocent game that brings a little harmless happiness to people's lives.

LIVE *LA BELLA VITA*
Give and Take

Encourage your man to give you attention and pay you compliments when he genuinely wants to say something nice to you. If you're embarrassed or worried about appearing too egotistical or needy, why not start by complimenting him first? Comment on the color of his shirt or his necktie, or his haircut, or the smell of his aftershave. There's always something you can praise—if not, why are you with the guy?

Eye Contact with a Partner (or Potential Partner!)

Try out some Italian-style eye contact. Hold your partner in a steady, unwavering gaze (*sguardo audace*) that shows interest and appreciation, though avoid coming across as arrogant or aggressive. People say good eye contact and a winning smile are the two basic ingredients to attracting someone's interest. Use facial expressions to reflect your total concentration on the person in front of you. Don't let your eyes wander. Lean in a little closer to him to demonstrate you're attentive and listening to what he's saying. And keep your body language open and receptive; don't cross your arms.

STARS IN THEIR EYES (*LE STELLE NEGLI OCCHI*)

It's thanks to the silver screen that people who have never even been to Italy are in love with the country. Italian movies and their stars have dazzled the world with stories of love affairs, passion, desire, frustration, intrigue, growing up, and getting married (or divorced); basically all the loving and living in the incredibly scenic backdrop that is the *bel paese*. Immortalized by both Italian and international directors filming scooter rides in Rome, gondola trips through Venice's canals, walks in the Tuscan woods, and car chases through the streets of Turin, images of Italy are still stamped on the world's collective imagination today. Because cinema often mirrors real life, watching Italian films can give you a good grasp of what is attractive to the Italian eye, and it offers plenty of ideas of how to recreate that image yourself. The following lists are by no means exhaustive; they're just a sample of what's out there. All the titles are either connected to love or are so beautifully shot or portrayed that they leave you aglow.

Buona visione! (Enjoy the show!)

RECENT ITALIAN MOVIES TO MAKE YOU SWOON

- *Io ballo da sola (Stealing Beauty)*, 1996, by Bernardo Bertolucci
- *La balia (The Nanny)*, 1999, by Marco Bellocchio

- *Pane e tulipani (Bread and Tulips)*, 2000, by Silvio Soldini
- *Malèna*, 2000, by Giuseppe Tornatore
- *L'ultimo bacio (The Last Kiss)*, 2001, by Gabriele Muccino
- *La finestra di fronte (Facing Windows)*, 2003, by Ferzan Ozpetek
- *La meglio gioventù (The Best of Youth)*, 2003, by Marco Tullio Giordana
- *Tre metri sopra il cielo (Three Steps Over Heaven)*, 2004, by Luca Lucini
- *Ho voglia di te (I Want You)*, 2007, by Luis Prieto (the sequel to *Three Steps*)
- *Manuale d'amore I e II (Love Manual 1 & 2)*, 2005 and 2007, by Giovanni Veronesi

CLASSIC ITALIAN MUST-SEE MOVIES

- *Cronaca di un amore (Story of a Love Affair)*, 1950, by Michelangelo Antonioni
- *Pane Amore e Fantasia (Bread, Love and Dreams)*, 1953, by Luigi Comencini
- *Le notti bianche (White Nights)*, 1957, by Luchino Visconti
- *La Dolce Vita*, 1960, by Federico Fellini
- *Ieri, oggi, domani (Yesterday, Today, and Tomorrow)*, 1963, by Vittorio De Sica
- *Matrimonio all'italiana (Marriage Italian Style)*, 1964, by Vittorio De Sica

- *Il giardino dei Finzi Contini* (*The Garden of the Finzi-Continis*), 1970, by Vittorio De Sica
- *Romeo e Giulietta* (*Romeo and Juliet*), 1968, by Franco Zeffirelli
- *Straziami, ma di baci saziami* (*Torture Me But Kill Me with Kisses*), 1968, by Dino Risi
- *Profumo di donna* (*Scent of a Woman*), 1974, by Dino Risi; remade in America in 1992 with Al Pacino in the starring role
- *Dramma della gelosia—tutti i particolari in cronaca* (*The Pizza Triangle*), 1970, by Ettore Scola
- *Travolti da un insolito destino nell'azzurro mare d'agosto* (*Swept Away*), 1974, by Lina Wertmuller
- *Una giornata particolare* (*A Special Day*), 1977, by Ettore Scola

Pietro Says

Yes, Italian men will look at and admire a woman's curves, but in reality, the thing that *ti fa scattare sono gli occhi* (really pulls your trigger is her eyes). They are the *specchio del suo desiderio* (the mirror of her desire). A woman's eyes reveal if she wants you or if she is willing to be courted by you. If *ti guarda male* (she gives you a dirty look), you know to change tack. If she gives an *occhietto* (a wink), the Italian male's attention is *al massimo* (at fever pitch). Nine times out of ten nothing will ever come of it; it's harmless, sexy fun. And if you do happen to come across that one-in-ten possibility when things may go farther, then all the better . . .

**POPULAR INTERNATIONAL MOVIES
MADE IN ITALY**

- *Quo Vadis*, 1951, by Mervyn LeRoy
- *Roman Holiday*, 1953, by William Wyler
- *Three Coins in the Fountain*, 1954, by Jean Negulesco
- *Summertime*, 1955, by David Lean
- *The Italian Job*, 1969, by Peter Collinson
- *A Room with a View*, 1985, by James Ivory
- *Il Postino (The Postman)*, 1994, by Michael Radford
- *The Talented Mr. Ripley*, 1999, by Anthony Minghella
- *Heaven*, 2002, by Tom Tykwer
- *Under the Tuscan Sun*, 2003, by Audrey Wells

Compliments to Your Mother (*Complimenti alla mamma*)

Italians use this phrase when pointing out someone's good looks, and certain legendary Italian stars of the silver screen are able to inspire and help us conjure a bit of that Italian-style sexy allure for ourselves (and our lovers). Here are some iconic Italian actors, known for both their suave good looks and their natural talents:

- **The Radiant Good Guy—Raoul Bova (1971–):** His handsome, boy-next-door looks combined with the svelte figure of a man who used to be a championship swimmer are further enhanced by his dedication to his wife and kids and his commitment to humanitarian causes.

- **The Spotlight Chaser—Vittorio Gassman (1922–2000):** He had a great ability to charm women with his stories and his magnetic gaze. He was a man of intense emotions, famous for his sense of humor and antiestablishment opinions. His reputation as a perfectionist meant he always cut an elegantly attired figure. Nicknamed *il mattatore* (the spotlight chaser) after the TV program that first brought him widespread popularity.

- **The Mercurial Charmer—Giancarlo Giannini (1942–):** This Oscar®-nominee's handsome, rugged looks are offset by his intense, mercurial eyes and melancholy charm. He excels at dialects and made a name for himself as a dubber, lending his voice to famous actors such as Al Pacino, Jack Nicholson, and Dustin Hoffman. His fluent English has enabled him to star in international productions outside Italy, such as the 2008 James Bond movie, *Quantum of Solace*.

- **The Latin Lover—Marcello Mastroianni (1924–1996):** He exuded elegance and style, charm and class, yet he considered himself to be "ordinary." His self-effacing nature meant he frequently tried to shy away from his reputation as a Latin lover to play characters who were sensitive or weak. He was internationally acclaimed for his multifaceted range as a performer, and among his physical attributes was a particularly sexy soft-spoken voice.

- **The Passionate Bad Boy—Riccardo Scamarcio (1979–):** One of the hottest sex symbols on the Italian scene today, his magnetism emanates from his sultry, dangerously gleaming half-hooded blue eyes, dark, wind-ruffled hair, and sexy stubble. Born in southern Italy, he subtly exudes the classic traits of the Italian male from that part of the country, coming across as something of a macho man who expects his woman to succumb to his every desire.

Women of the Italian Silver Screen

These Italian divas are emblematic actresses dripping with style and sex appeal:

- **The Kick-Ass Chick—Asia Argento (1975–):** She has frequently played at being the "dark lady", outrageously flirty yet tough. But don't be fooled by her tattoos, punk clothes, and seemingly riotous, unconventional lifestyle: she is one smart, hard-working cookie, performing in English, French, and Italian as well as being a film director, novelist, and DJ. She is the daughter of the famous horror movie director, Dario Argento, but Asia is most definitely her own woman, not afraid to stand up for herself or to fight against being stereotyped.

- **The Classic Italian Beauty—Monica Bellucci (1964–):** Her name frequently appears ranking high in lists of the sexiest women in the world. She is a classic Italian beauty with long, flowing dark hair, sultry eyes, and a curvaceous figure that she is not afraid to show off. She was first seen on the catwalks before she moved onto the big screen, and is completely comfortable with herself (she admits she likes to eat: "Who cares? I'm natural," she says), though she always presents a highly polished, sophisticated image. She brims with inner confidence.

- **The Athletic Bond Girl—Caterina Murino (1977–):** Her rise to international silver screen stardom was cemented in 2006 when she bagged the part of Bond girl Solange in *Casino Royale* with Daniel Craig. This bewitchingly beautiful young woman, with an exquisite figure and long, sinewy legs, originally wanted to be a doctor. After failing to get into medical school, she placed fourth in the Miss Italy contest, started a modeling career, then studied acting, performing on stage and for the big screen. Her athleticism is evident in her passion for dancing tango and flamenco.

- **The Natural—Valeria Golino (1966–):** Her curly hair, sparkling blue eyes and *acqua e sapone* appearance (literally soap and water, meaning natural) have combined with this former model's talent as an actress to build up a solid career in Italy and in Hollywood (for example, she played the love interest opposite Tom

Cruise in *Rain Man* and starred with Charlie Sheen in *Hot Shots*). She has a tendency to be self-deprecating, though she is very intelligent, and she has a great sense of humor. After dating Benicio Del Toro, Valeria's wholesome yet sexy charms have now won over heartthrob Riccardo Scarmarcio, and together they make a truly hot couple.

- **The Legend—Sophia Loren (1934–):** This international screen goddess has always attributed her tremendous strength of character, ability to appreciate life, and determination to succeed to the extreme poverty she experienced as a child living in the slums outside Naples. She has given maximum expression to so much of life's pleasure and pain, with an unusual mix of weakness and power, fragility, and control. For the film *Volver*, Penélope Cruz used Sophia as an archetypal role model of motherhood from the Golden Age of Italian cinema, mimicking her physicality, principally the way she swayed her hips when she walked.

KEY PHRASES FOR SIGHT

Come sei elegante oggi.	You look very elegant today.
Andiamo a fare una passeggiata in centro?	Shall we go for a walk downtown?
Che figura!	How embarrassing!
Mettiti un po' di trucco.	Put a little makeup on.
Perchè non provi quelle scarpe con un'altra gonna?	Why don't you try those shoes with a different skirt?
Stai bene in quel vestito.	You look nice in that dress.
Vado a vedere le passerelle a Milano.	I'm going to see the fashion shows in Milan.
Mi piace essere alla moda.	I like wearing the latest fashion.
É una vera fatica seguire la moda.	It's really hard work keeping up with the latest fashions.
Questi tacchi sono troppo alti.	These heels are too high.
Andiamo al cinema!	Let's go to the movies!
Preferisci sedere avanti o indietro?	Do you prefer to sit at the front or the back?
Il mio attore italiano / la mia attrice italiana preferito/a è . . .	My favorite Italian actor / actress is . . .

TWO

SWEET NOTHINGS

Sussurri d'amore

The sound of the Italian language is simply enchanting. People are mesmerized and beguiled by its melodic tones and rhythmic cadences, which, to foreign ears, can lend a mysterious and romantic air even to something as mundane as a shopping list. Spoken communication is fundamental for Italians, whether in face-to-face or cell phone conversations. They have a highly attuned ear and have developed their love of music into a refined tradition, covering the spectrum from opera to rock. Let's tune your *udito* (hearing) to a more Italian frequency.

DID YOU KNOW ?

In Rome, Gregorian chanting concerts are often performed in ancient abbeys or Roman cloisters. These large vaulted halls are a perfect location for the heavenly music, which echoes all around, engulfing and enfolding you in its divine melodies—as well as for a romantic, Sunday morning date.

THE SOUND OF *PAROLE DOLCI* (SWEET WORDS)

Italian is a very flowery and overblown language, filled with highly polished flourishes, long-winded phrases, and *sfumatura* (subtle nuances). Indeed, you often hear a lot of *aria fritta*, which translates as "fried air" and means "hot air." You should absolutely learn some basic Italian if you are planning to spend some time in Italy, but even if you're staying at home, it is a beautiful language to study—words are simply more beautiful when spoken in *italiano*.

DID YOU KNOW ?

Italians are not afraid to raise their voices, but they are careful not to interfere with cooking. We once heard two Italian guys screaming and bellowing at each other, arguing about politics. All of a sudden, in midsentence, one turned to the other and said, "Shhhhh, otherwise the soufflé will drop"—only in Italy!

A PASSION TO SHOUT ABOUT

You can always spot a group of Italians in a crowd, not purely because of their elegant and flamboyant attire, but also because of the noise they generate. They must be among the loudest people on the planet, doing everything with zest, passion, and a love of life—all at the top of their lungs. It's fair to say Italians are not good at *sottovoce* (speaking softly).

To foreign ears, the sound of Italians arguing, screaming, and shouting tirades at ear-splitting volumes can be quite daunting, if not downright scary. If you heard similar noise levels at home, you'd be concerned there was trouble brewing, particularly when accompanied by aggressive body language such as puffed-up chests, pointing fingers, and the like. But in Italy, this extreme form of vocal sparring, often paired with strings of pithy insults, is not personal, it's just Italians venting or passionately expressing their opinions and feelings. They are very forceful and persuasive in their use of language. Let's look at some of the occasions where Italians are likely to yell.

DID YOU KNOW ?

If you search out movies on DVD with Italian offered as a language option (the ideal is to have a choice of both Italian audio and subtitles), you can hear how the film sounds in Italian while reading the English subtitles to aid comprehension, or vice versa. For people whose Italian is rusty, this is a great way to get back up to speed and is an enjoyable "subliminal" vocabulary lesson.

In Arguments with Friends and Family

Sometimes when Italians are yelling, they really *are* fighting! Italians use deafening shouting matches as a way of clearing the air, which they see as essential to any disagreement. Verbal battles are considered a healthy way to liberate harbored resentment, giving both parties the opportunity to vent and air their grievances and frustrations (albeit at high decibel levels).

While we don't advocate insulting people in Italian, you may hear some of these terms while in the company of disputing Italians:

Coglione	Twit/fool
Idiota	Idiot
Pezzente	Loser
Cretino	Jerk
Stronzo/a!	Shit
Puttana/mignotta/troia	Bitch/slut /whore
Testa di cazzo	Dickhead
Bastardo	Bastard

If you're brave enough, try the Italian method of arguing at full volume. You may find it cathartic because you'll rid yourself of negative feelings in a hurry!

In Arguments with Lovers

Virtually all couples fight at some point, but Italians have a unique view of the benefits of "yell therapy." In fact, Italian couples actually enjoy a good shouting match, and, while it may seem contradictory, they believe that having a good argument is actually one of the most intimate things you can do with your partner.

Why? Having a good old row is not only passionate, but it can also offer the prospect for genuine change, something not always easy to achieve through lengthy negotiation and reasoned discussion.

While adopting the full-blown Italian approach to your quarrels may make you unpopular with your neighbors, refining your arguing skills can have a beneficial effect on your relationship, especially if you're someone who usually shies away from a dispute. Follow the tactics of Italian women: don't be afraid of confrontation, learn how to hold your own in an argument, and be sure if you dish it out, you can take it too. Your partner may treat you with more respect in the future. Then, of course, it's always great to kiss and make up afterwards . . .

DID YOU KNOW ?

Italian is classified as one of the Romance languages within the Indo-European family, and is mainly derived from Latin, as are Spanish, French, and Portuguese. Modern-day Italian is based on the Tuscan vernacular, which came to dominate Italy's many other dialects thanks to Tuscany's central position and the role of its regional capital Florence as a center for trade and culture. This dialect started its ascent in the fourteenth century, and was popularized by famous authors living and working in Tuscany, such as Dante Alighieri (*The Divine Comedy*), Francesco Petrarch (known for his love poetry), and Giovanni Boccaccio (*The Decameron*). However, it was only after the unification of Italy, in 1861, that this dialect was adopted as the new nation's universal tongue.

When Celebrating

Making a commotion is also an integral part of Italian celebrations, which aren't seen as true parties unless the noise is ratcheted up to the highest possible level. Every key event has some noise-related accompaniment: weddings, sporting victories, and even funerals (where the custom is to clap as the coffin passes). But *calcio* (soccer), Italy's national obsession, is one of the loudest noise generators, whether in or out of the stadium. If you have ever been in an Italian town when the local team has won, you have probably seen the streams of cars packed with flag-waving fans blaring air horns out of the windows, and people riding around on *motorini* (scooters) singing and chanting. Live the Italian way: If you're celebrating something, why not share your joy with the world?

Pietro Says

Try to explicitly tell your lover what you do and don't like in bed—not in a schoolmarm way, but by gently steering him in the right direction. If that is too difficult, at least don't stifle your *gemiti* (moans of pleasure); they can be just as good a guide for the attentive lover. Like the accomplished Italian lover, sharpen your awareness and learn to spot the variations in your partner's reactions: listen for the differences between sighs of pleasure and those of frustration, or even—heaven forbid—boredom. If you follow these signs, you will probably soon notice improvement in your lovemaking.

In Bed

One final area of Italian life where noise matters is the bedroom. As you can imagine, Italians are not buttoned up and silent when making love—they tend to be highly vocal in the throes of pleasure. This verbal passion helps drum up excitement and heighten arousal. It is an undeniable physical sign that you're enjoying yourself. Give it a try with your partner! If you're not used to it, it may seem strange at first. But keep with it and you could well find it transports you and your partner to even greater sexual heights.

These are a few basic Italian terms used in the bedroom. Don't use them with everyone—they are pretty vulgar. Strictly for lovers only!

Il cazzo	Dick
La fica	Pussy
Il culo	Ass
Le tette	Tits
I capezzoli	Nipples
Il collo	Neck
Le gambe	Legs
Le orecchie	Ears
Le cosce	Thighs
Sono ancora vergine.	I'm still a virgin.
Mi piace fare l'amore con te.	I like making love with you.
Mi ecciti da morire.	You really turn me on.
Amo dormire con te.	I love sleeping with you.

Con te il sesso è sublime.	Sex is wonderful with you.
Voglio morderti l'orecchio.	I want to bite your ear.
Fammi godere!	Make me come! (lit: Give me pleasure!)
Sei proprio un/a porco/a.	You're really dirty.
Mi piace quando mi tocchi lì.	I like it when you touch me there.
Gli italiani lo fanno meglio!	Italians do it better!

GOSSIPING

Being an inherently curious—ahem, nosey—lot, Italians adore standing around gossiping and will always find time for a *chiacchierata* (quick chat). They are "people people," placing a high priority on fostering and nurturing human contact with everyone in their lives. For Italians, any location is perfect to talk, whether in the *piazza*, at the bar, in the store, on the street corner, or in the yard, chatting to your neighbor as you hang the laundry out to dry. You don't have to exchange malicious gossip to appreciate the joys of catching up on news and events in the lives of those around you.

As you will see in Chapter Five, one of the prime topics of conversation is food, but Italians also love to talk politics (discussions that frequently degenerate into high-decibel shouting matches); relationships and sex; the weather; and the perennial favorite: traffic-related topics such as holdups, parking problems, and the best shortcuts to take. Whatever the subject, Italians love sharing their knowledge with others, so if you listen carefully to their conversations you can quickly pick up tips on where to find the tastiest artisan *gelato* in town or how to find the quickest route from point A to point B.

DID YOU KNOW ?

Words reflect attitudes. In Italy, someone who cheats on their partner may be labeled *edonista* (a hedonist) rather than promiscuous. Indeed, Italians were rather puzzled when the "Monicagate" scandal broke in America. Their take on it was "what goes on behind closed doors is their business, not ours"; though, being intrinsically nosey, the Italians were more than happy to hear all the salacious details. However, Clinton's infidelity certainly did not compromise the then–American president's reputation in Italian eyes. This may explain the low-key Italian reaction to the allegations of sex scandals surrounding their own prime minister, Silvio Berlusconi.

GIVING COMPLIMENTS

While Italians enjoy a little gossip here and there, they also make time to compliment others. Because they are always checking each other out, they are quick to notice details such as a new pair of shoes or a different hairstyle.

How can you give some compliments, Italian style? Try out these phrases:

Ciao bella!	Hey, babe! (Hi, good looking!)
Che begli occhi che hai.	What beautiful eyes you have.
Oggi stai proprio in forma.	You're looking fit / in good shape today.
Quanto sei bella!	You're so beautiful!
Che buon profumo che hai.	You smell nice.
Che bella abbronzatura.	What a great tan.
Ammazza! Stai proprio bene con quel vestito.	Wow! You look really great in that dress.

THE BENEFITS OF REALLY LISTENING

In addition to being good talkers, Italians are acute listeners, whether the person speaking is a significant other or a passing acquaintance. When Italians ask you *com'è stai?* (How are you doing?), they actually pay attention to your reply; it's not just a mere formality. There is a big difference between the reply *bene* (well, good) and *benino* (quite well), *benone* (great), *non bene* (not good), and *male* (bad). If your answer is anything other than *bene*, Italians will follow up their initial question with *come mai? Che ti è successo?* (How come? What happened to you?) They want to know what's wrong—or right.

Ask yourself if you listen with this much intensity, or if you barely notice someone's response to the quick "Hello, how are you?" question. Showing a genuine interest in the answer shows you actually do care about what the person is saying and that you're paying attention to his or her feelings, emotions, and moods. Honing your listening skills to a heightened Italian wavelength can reap untold rewards in all your relationships with your partner, family, or friends.

DID YOU KNOW ?

About 70 million people speak Italian, most of whom are in Italy, though it is spoken in San Marino, parts of Switzerland, and Vatican City, as well as areas of Slovenia and Croatia. The language is also well known in Monaco, Malta, Corsica, Nice, and Albania. If you travel around Italy you will find regional dialects are still widely spoken, though people do understand and speak "regular" Italian.

ACCENTUATE THE POSITIVE

Italians are very imaginative in their use of words. When talking about someone's physical attributes, they often put a positive spin on things and emphasize beauty rather than using language to denigrate (though this obviously depends on who they're talking about and their relationship with that person). For example: In America, someone with a big nose may be described as having a "schnoz," which is considered a putdown or even a slur. In Italy, that person would be said to have a *naso importante* (an important nose).

Another example: Clothes for fuller-figured people are called *taglie forti* (strong sizes).

> ### LIVE *LA BELLA VITA*
> #### *Be Proud of What You Have*
> Our American friend was with an older Italian guy, who was virtually bald with the classic "three hairs" sticking out of his head. He grabbed our friend's hand and said "close your eyes, *senti* [feel this]," as he brushed her fingers along his remaining strands. She thought, "What are you so proud of? They're three hairs, for goodness's sake!" As if he heard her, he said: "*Pura seta!*" (pure silk). Unlike a lot of men, he was not at all embarrassed or ashamed by his baldness, rather, he was fiercely proud of what (little) he had. Follow his lead—be proud of yourself!

Taking this positive approach to language makes you view things in a different light, and also generates different reactions from those around you. In Italy, people are constantly given the message "you're beautiful the way you are," thus engendering self-confidence, whereas in America, the implication is often "You've got something wrong; we'll fix you," which can obviously have the opposite effect. So the next time you want to say something negative, choose an Italian way of saying it for a more constructive impact.

WHISPERING SWEET NOTHINGS IN ITALIAN

Of all the subjects to talk about in Italian, love may be the most beautiful and thrilling. Even if your Italian language skills are not up to proclamations of lengthy poetic phrases, it is nevertheless pretty easy to add an exotic twist to your loving linguistic repertoire simply by using an Italian nickname for your lover or judiciously adding the occasional short Italian phrase into your speech.

With a Lover

If you're in a relationship, try to work in some Italian words and phrases here and there to spice things up. Whether you're asking him to take out the trash or join you in the bedroom, your request will be so much sexier if you use an Italian pet name! And of course, he should start using them as well . . .

To start you off, here are some loving nicknames in Italian:

Bello/a (mio/mia)	Beauty (mine)
Amore mio	My love / Darling
Tesoro	Treasure
Passerotto/a	Little sparrow
Fiorellino	Little flower
Principessa	Princess
Coccolino/a	Darling (literally, little cuddle)
Micetta	Little kitten (used for women only)

YOUR *PARADISO*

CYCLING TRIPS

The more energetic tourist may wish to plan a cycling (or motor-bike) trip to experience the joys of Italian nature close at hand: riding past fields of sunflowers, olive groves, orchards, and vineyards provides an unparalleled sensory overload and a host of memories to treasure forever. Everyone has heard of the beauties of Tuscany, with its charming hilltop towns, rolling green countryside, and fabulous food. But if you want to go a bit off the beaten track, try Umbria or Abruzzo, or the untouched landscapes and natural parks in Calabria and Apulia (Puglia in Italian), where you will find the curious round houses called *trulli*. For a truly spectacular vision of man working in harmony with nature, head to Matera in Basilicata, a magical cluster of hundreds of cave churches carved into the rocks (known as the *Parco delle Chiese Rupestri del Materano*, one Italy's many UNESCO-listed world heritage sites, also used as an international film location), offering uplifting inspiration for all who visit.

Here is a selection of key expressions for lovers:

Ti voglio bene. (abbrev: *TVB*)	I like / love you (Note: this phrase is used liberally to express affection, not only between lovers but also with friends and family. While it can mean "I love you" when spoken by a girl/boyfriend, it carries less "weight" than the next phrase on our list).
Ti amo.	I love you. [The *real thing*!]
Mi manchi.	I miss you.
Desidero vederti.	I really want to see you.
Sono pazzo/a di te!	I'm crazy about you!
Tra noi, un colpo di fulmine!	For us, it was love at first sight!
Siamo proprio innamorati!	We're both really in love!
Sto proprio bene con te.	I feel really good with you (you make me feel really good).
Stiamo bene insieme.	We're good together.
Ho voglia di te!	I want you!
Mi vuoi sposare?	Do you want to marry me?
Ci sposiamo!	We're getting married!

Remember to use the Italians' smoldering eye contact to add extra oomph to your Italian words and phrases.

With a Potential Lover

Even if you are not yet in a relationship, you may want to add some Italian phrases to your repertoire. Be careful, though: as with using any foreign language, in the wrong context you may sound fake, corny, or downright pretentious.

Vuoi essere il mio (la mia) ragazzo(a)?	Do you want to be my boyfriend (girlfriend)?
Vuoi venire a cena con me?	Would you like to go out to dinner with me?
Quando possiamo incontrarci?	When can we meet?
Voglio vederti di nuovo.	I want to see you again.
Ti presento il mio (la mia) ragazzo(a).	Meet my boyfriend (girlfriend).
Questo è il mio (la mia) fidanzato(a).	This is my fiancé (fiancée).
Ti accompagno a casa?	Can I take you home?
Mi fai salire?	Can I come in?
Vieni a dormire da me?	Will you come back to sleep at my place? (This means for a platonic sleepover, but it could mean more depending on the look you give the person when you say it!)
Andiamo a letto!	Let's go to bed!

How Italian Men Flirt

Italian men often cut to the chase in a very immediate, if sometimes sleazy, way. Many Italian women tell stories of men who greet them for the first time by saying *"Io ti amo, ti voglio sposare!"* ("I love you, I want to marry you!"). After experiencing this direct approach more than once, women have perfected replies along the lines of *"grazie, ma cominciamo giusto con un caffè . . ."* ("well, thanks, but let's just start by having a coffee first . . ."). While we wouldn't suggest that anyone go quite this far, you might certainly take a page out of the Italians' book and be a bit more outgoing, taking the initiative more instead of seeing someone you fancy and not saying anything.

Pietro Says

Even if you don't speak Italian, you can still communicate in the universally understood "language of love"; for example, by declaring your affection with a kiss. However, you probably want to go further and actually converse with other people, or at least understand what they're saying to you. Here's an idea: Date an Italian speaker! Some claim the best way to learn a language is *a letto, non nell'aula* (in the bedroom, not the classroom). Spending large chunks of time with a lover who talks to you in Italian increases the likelihood that some of it will sink in.

When trying to pick up women, Italian men are exceedingly good at the patter—they come out with all sorts of romantic phrases to try to woo women. It brings a richness to women's lives, and makes them feel more appreciated and feminine. But Italian men don't just bombard women with words, they carefully judge their reaction too, varying their approach depending on the feedback they give them, whether verbally or through body language. The Italian man will test the waters to see which tack is most suited to the woman in front of him.

THE BEAUTIFUL SOUNDS OF ITALIAN MUSIC

Music is a fundamental part of Italian life, and Italy has made a huge contribution to the world's musical arts over the millennia. Everyone knows at least one Italian refrain, whether it's from an operatic aria or a romantic love song from Naples. Italian music can make your soul soar, your heart break, or your thoughts yearn for lazy hot summer days under the Mediterranean sun. Whatever your personal tastes, Italy's music has something for everyone, and there are many ways to introduce some Italian melody into your life. Here are some of the major categories of music and some famous Italian artists to check out.

Opera

One of the first kinds of music people associate with Italy is opera (called *opera lirica* in Italian). Italy's most famous opera writers are veritable cultural icons: Verdi, Rossini, Puccini, Donizetti, and Bellini. They captured the concerns of Italian society in the nineteenth and early twentieth centuries, using sweeping stories populated by "real-life" characters. More often than not, their love stories come to a tragic end, but the music charting those tragedies is sublime.

Italian composers employed the tradition of *bel canto* (beautiful singing), creating vocal pieces with long, flowery phrases allowing the singers to display their sophisticated vocal skills. Italy has produced some of the world's greatest opera singers: Enrico Caruso, Luciano Pavarotti, Mario Lanza (actually born in the United States to a family of Italian immigrants), Beniamino Gigli, and the current international star and "fourth tenor," Andrea Bocelli. Italian women have also lit up the opera stage, including great soprano Licia Albanese, rising star Sonia Ganassi, and the current darling, Cecilia Bartoli (discovered on a TV talent show).

Pietro Says

To *conquistare una donna* (win a woman over), Italian men understand that you must first conquer her *cervello* (her brain). While there are times for serious discussions or even full-blown, pot-throwing arguments, Italian men know the importance of making their woman *ridere e sognare* (laugh and dream). If not, things can become *molto pesante* (very heavy); laughter enriches the soul. This applies not only to your partner but to other people too. Who doesn't feel a buzz upon receiving a compliment or enjoying a good laugh?

Romantic operas sung in Italian are particularly stunning. Try to find versions sung by Italians, or conducted by famous Italian maestros, such as Arturo Toscanini or Riccardo Muti, who took over as music director of the Chicago Symphony Orchestra in 2008 (though he may be returning to Rome at the end of 2010).

You may not recognize the Italian titles of the following pieces, but when you hear the evocative excerpts, they will probably sound familiar.

- **Vincenzo Bellini (1801–1835):** *Casta Diva* from *Norma*
- **Gaetano Donizetti (1797–1848):** *Una furtiva lagrima* from *L'Elisir d'Amore*
- **Giacomo Puccini (1858–1924):** *Addio Fiorito Asil, Bimba Dagli Occhi,* and *Un Bel Di, Vedremo* from *Madama Butterfly; Vissi d'Arte, E lucevan le stelle, Recondita armonia* from *Tosca; Che gelida manina, Quando Me'n Vo'soletta per la Via, Si mi chiamo Mimi* from *La Bohème; Nessun dorma!* from *Turandot;* and *Ch'ella mi creda libero e lontano* from *La Fanciulla del West*
- **Gioacchino Rossini (1792–1868):** *Una voce poco fa* from *Il barbiere di Siviglia*
- **Giuseppe Verdi (1813–1901):** *Ave Maria* from *Otello; Celeste Aida* from *Aida; Caro Nome Che il Mio Cor* and *La donna è mobile* from *Rigoletto; Sempre Libre, E strano . . . Ah forse è lui,* and *Addio del Passato* from *La Traviata*
- **Pietro Mascagni (1863–1945):** *Mamma, quel vino è generoso* from *Cavalleria Rusticana*

While Italy boasts some of the greatest opera houses in the world—La Scala in Milan, the Fenice in Venice, and the Verona Arena in an outdoor ancient Roman amphitheatre, to name just a few—you don't have to travel that far to hear stirring Italian operas performed live. And tickets are not always out-of-reach expensive, either. Opera houses often hold cheaper matinee performances and offer last-minute deals or two-for-one packages. Check out a venue near you for a magnificent musical treat.

Rafter Raisers

If you prefer a good sing-along, you'll find plenty of popular Italian refrains in the international music consciousness:

1. A prime example is the Neapolitan *O Sole Mio*, a eulogy to love sung by a man looking up at a woman in a window on a bright sunny day after a storm, singing "your face is my sunshine" (in Italian, "*O sole mio sta in fronte a te*"). You can find it sung in Neapolitan or Italian and there are English language versions too—although the Elvis Presley hit *It's Now or Never* used the original music, but was not a translation of the Neapolitan text.

2. While not Italian, there is another song set in Naples, "where love is king," that rouses people to bellow out the final line of the chorus. You've surely heard it before: "When the moon hits your eye, like a big-a pizza pie . . ." Of course you know it—"That's amore!," the song most closely associated with American crooner Dean Martin.

These and other rollicking "organ-grinder" tunes will get your voice amped up to a more Italian volume.

ITALIAN SONGS TO SING IN THE SHOWER!
- *Arrivederci Roma*
- *Funiculì, Funiculà*
- *Innammorata*
- *Mattinata*
- *Non Dimenticar*
- *O Sole Mio*
- *Quando Quando Quando*
- *That's Amore*
- *Torna a Surriento*
- *Volare (nel blu dipinto di blu)*

Other Italian Music

Italy has many other flourishing music scenes, from pop to rock, folk to political songs, ballet music to Gregorian chanting. There is a particularly strong tradition of singer-songwriters, known as *cantautori*, who have penned many of Italy's favorite love songs. Then there are the great Italian composers for the silver screen, including Ennio Morricone (*Once Upon a Time in the West, The Mission*); Nicola Piovani (*Life Is Beautiful*); and the relatively new kid on the block, Dario Marianelli, who recently won an Oscar for his soundtrack to *Atonement*.

If you like to dance, search out some traditional music from the Italian regions, such as the famous tarantella, a rhythmic ritual folk dance often played at weddings. Popular legend claims it was invented as a way of extracting the poison caused by tarantula spider bites.

LIVE *LA BELLA VITA*
Sing a Lover's Serenade

From wedding songs to apologetic refrains that help make up after a fight, the Italian tradition of serenades is about as romantic as it gets. Professional serenaders operate in some Italian cities, crooning to their client's beloved (who is lit up in their window with a portable spotlight), using amplifiers to make their music heard above the traffic noise. You don't have to go that far, but if you have the courage (and doesn't love make everyone feel invincible?), learn a romantic Italian love song and then pluck your partner's heartstrings by singing it to him or her from the street. It may sound schmaltzy, but it will certainly be something he or she—and the people who witness your performance—will remember forever.

CONTEMPORARY ITALIAN MUSICIANS AND GROUPS

- Fabrizio de André: Rock and Traditional
- Lucio Battisti: Melodic and Rock
- Alex Britti: Pop and Blues

- Riccardo Cocciante: Pop and Orchestral
- Pino Daniele: Neapolitan rock
- Giorgia: Pop and Jazz
- Jovanotti: Rap
- Luciano Ligabue: Pop
- Mina: Cross-genre
- Morgan: Pop
- Negroamaro: Pop / Rock
- Laura Pausini: Pop
- Eros Ramazzotti: Pop
- Subsonica: Electronic dance
- Zucchero: Pop, Rock, and Blues

If you're a karaoke fan, hunt down some Italian songs as a fun way of practicing your pronunciation with family and friends.

LIVE *LA BELLA VITA*
Sing to Your Babies

Sing an Italian lullaby or *ninna-nanna* to send your young children drifting off into peaceful slumber. Some popular examples are *Stella Stellina, Fai la Nanna, Mio Simone, Farfallina,* and *Fate la nanna, coscine di pollo,* which literally means "Go to sleep, little chicken legs!"

I JUST CALLED TO SAY . . .

People in Italy are just plain crazy about their cell phones, referred to as a *telefonino* ("little telephone") or *cellulare*. According to Research and Markets, Italy has one of Europe's most vibrant cellular markets, estimated as worth 27.3 billion euros at the end of 2006, far above the European average, with 74.5 million subscribers making up 128 percent (!) of the total population—basically meaning Italy has more cell phones than people. Italians are incessant callers and text-messagers, always ready to find a little time (and money) to contact you by phone.

Talking on the Phone

Here's a script for a very basic phone conversation in Italian . . .

Pronto (when answering)	Hello?
Ciao! (when replying)	Hi!
Com' è stai?	How are you?
Bene grazie, e tu?	I'm fine, and you?
Ci vediamo più tardi?	Shall we meet up later?
Si, dove?	Yep, where?
Al solito posto nel centro?	At our usual place downtown?
Va bene. Ci vediamo li alle 8.	Okay. See you there at eight.
Magari dopo troviamo un posto per mangiare?	Then perhaps we can find somewhere to eat?
Perfetto. Ciao, a dopo.	Perfect. Bye, see you later.

Cell Phones and Relationships

Italians primarily use cell phones to keep in touch with friends and family members, but as in the United States, cell phone conversations are ubiquitous in romantic relationships. In fact, more than 43 percent of cell usage in Italy is between spouses or partners, who know that maintaining a simmering level of passion keeps loved ones from straying (figures from the 2006 report into "the use of media and cell phones in Italy," published by ISTAT, the Italian National Institute of Statistics). If an Italian is thinking about you during the day, he'll make the effort to give you a quick call—something worth emulating in your own relationships with your spouse, family members, or friends. Though you may not want to imitate the frequency of calls: lovers will often ring you again half an hour after your last chat, just to make sure you're still thinking about them—or perhaps they're just checking up on you, monitoring your every move!

By the same token, cell phones are *also* frequently used to conduct secret affairs and it is not uncommon to see Italian men with two or even three different *telefonini* (one for the family, one for work, and one for the mistress). And, like everyone who uses a cell for an illicit liaison, Italians have learned the hard way that it can be a *traditore* (traitor), riddled with dangerous traces of phone calls and messages. For the careless or unaware, cell phones have increased the chances of uncovering infidelity. As a result, many Italians have become adept at deleting call logs and text messages to cover their tracks.

Another, often cheaper way of communicating with friends or lovers via your cell is to send a message rather than call. While not strictly related to the theme of "hearing," sending your partner a loving text message (referred to by Italians as an *SMS*, using the English acroymn for Short Message Service) or the now increasingly popular picture messages (*MMS* in Italian, from Multimedia Messaging Service) via your cell is a simple, concise, and undemanding way to show affection. Some people fill their texts with literary quotes or poetry, and, ever quick to spot a business opportunity, there are now plenty of Italian websites with screeds of ready-made phrases for every occasion to add a touch of finesse to your texting. The text message is now also becoming increasingly common in the Italian administrative domain; for example, texts are used to confirm train reservations, payment for parking, or to provide information such as the varying prices for basic foodstuffs around the country to consumers.

Pietro Says

My American friend was hit on by an Italian guy and they agreed to meet up later for a date. She gave him her *numero di cellulare* (cell number) and they parted. After going only a few feet, while still in range of sight, her phone rang. It was the guy, saying "*Mi manchi gia!*" ("I'm missing you already!"). She thought this was very sweet and charming and was rather disillusioned when I pointed out that he was probably just checking to be sure she hadn't given him the wrong number!

Text messaging remains prevalent among young Italians, possibly because it is cheaper than calling (for example, according to ISTAT, text messaging is the main function used on the cell phone by 70.1 percent of users between the ages of eleven and fourteen, with a high of 80.1 percent for the fifteen to seventeen age group). As in the rest of the world, Italians use emoticons to speed up texting and they have also developed their own forms of abbreviations, such as *TVB* (abbreviation of *ti voglio bene*, I love you) or TVTB (abbreviation of *ti voglio tanto bene*, I love you so much).

KEY PHRASES FOR HEARING

Parli l'italiano?	Do you speak Italian?
Parlo poco l'italiano, ma lo capisco.	I don't speak much Italian, but I understand it.
Parli più lentamente per favore.	Please speak slower.
Ti piace questa musica?	Do you like this music?
Vuoi andare ad un concerto?	Do you want to go to a concert?
Mi piace l'opera lirica.	I like opera.
Ti chiamo dopo sul cell.	I'll call you later on your cell phone.
Dov'è il mio telefonino? L'hai visto?	Where's my cell phone? Have you seen it?
Andiamo allo stadio a vedere la partita?	Shall we go to the stadium to watch the (soccer) game?
Forza Roma! (Juve, Napoli, etc.)	Go for it, Roma! (substitute with a team of your choice).

YOUR *PARADISO*

ART CITIES

There is a huge array of ravishing art cities for tourists to visit: Pisa and its leaning tower; Verona with its Roman amphitheatre (also great for a "treasure hunt" in search of the balcony where Romeo declared his love to Juliet—The one thought to be the original is now available to rent for weddings if you want to tie the knot Italian style); Milan with the magnificent Duomo cathedral and Da Vinci's *Last Supper* (and a place for some serious shopping); Turin with its visually striking Mole Antonelliana landmark standing at almost 550 feet (the city is also packed with expert Tarot card readers for those who fancy looking into the future); Genoa and its bustling port (not surprising in the birthplace of Columbus); Bologna with its medieval brick buildings and porticoed streets; and Perugia, Italy's chocolate-making center.

Just south of Naples is the world renowned Costiera Amalfitana (Amalfi coast), a magnificent panoramic coastline dotted with villages precariously perched on the sea cliffs. Perhaps Italy's ultimate romantic holiday destination, this area has attracted composers, artists, writers, and film stars: Edward Grieg, J.M.W. Turner, Joan Miró, Tennessee Williams, Greta Garbo, Clark Gable, and Humphrey Bogart, to name but a few. Visual gems include Ravello (Gore Vidal is a current resident), offering breathtaking panoramas from fertile gardens; Positano, a chic resort built on terraces carved into the hills, with white Moorish houses descending to the sea; and the historic town of Amalfi, with buildings that bear witness to its past role as a major seafaring power. Smaller villages such as Minori, Maiori, and Praiano are also charming and picturesque, and are usually quieter if you're looking for a more intimate experience. For the brave at heart, rent a car and drive (slowly) along the infamous and pretty scary coastal road with its hairpin bends and fantastic views of the sea below. If you do decide to go for it, the best advice to reduce the overall stomach-churning effect generated by sheer hundred-foot drops to the water is to travel it from South to North; that way, you are driving hugging the mountain, not driving along the sea side. To calm your nerves after your trip, sample a glass of the famous local liqueur called *limoncello*, made from the lemons that grow here in abundance.

THREE

A LOVING TOUCH

Un tocco d'amore

Italians are renowned for being very tactile, and having a highly developed sense of *tatto* (touch). When they communicate, they even add touch to their words to emphasize their message. This chapter examines some of the specific ways Italians use physical contact as a means of expression—whether in friendship or in love—and how you can adopt this touch in your own life.

Pietro Says

The Italians' idea of personal space is much more narrow than what Americans are used to. Some men will try to *approffitare un po'* (take a bit of advantage) when greeting a woman they like with a double kiss. The *bacio* (kiss) can end up being rather close to the *bocca* (mouth) rather than smack in the middle of the cheek. But on the whole, Italian men are pretty attentive, carefully watching out for signals from women to gauge if they are pushing things too far.

CLOSE ENCOUNTERS OF THE ITALIAN KIND

If you ever partake in the delightful sport of people-watching while sitting sipping a coffee in an Italian *piazza*, apart from their immediately apparent stylish elegance, you will notice a lot of physical contact between people, whether they are lovers, friends, or acquaintances. This is something that really stands out for Americans, who don't touch the way Italians do. Some Americans may even be shocked or offended by the inordinate amount of invasion of personal space that goes on in Italy. But things need to be put in context; in Italian society, light, affectionate touching is much more acceptable—*anzi* (on the contrary), it's the norm rather than the exception.

Perhaps all this touching and familiarity with other people's bodies stems from the fact that Italians spend a lot of time together at the beach, semi-naked in their swim gear. You'll often see friends of both sexes preening each other under the sun. Even if they are not seaside, they are probably still dressed lightly, given Italy's balmy climate. So tactile exposure to bare flesh is a more natural and common experience with less social stigma attached to it in Italy than in the United States.

DID YOU KNOW ?

One form of touching that is much less pleasant to be on the receiving end of is the old Italian habit of "rear pinching" (known as *la mano morta*, literally translated as the "dead hand") on public transportation, which got to a point where some tourist bus routes became notorious for such incidents. Fortunately, this nasty and sordid practice is becoming much more a thing of the past as the Italian courts are now getting tough in cases of "wandering hands."

Women will "groom" men, smoothing down their hair, or gently stroking their arms (even if they're not partners). You will see women friends strolling hand-in-hand and men throwing their arms around each other or walking down the street linking arms, without a hint of self-consciousness. In Italy, men touching is not seen as a threat to masculinity—in fact, quite the reverse; it actually confirms a man is comfortable with his sexuality.

DID YOU KNOW ?

Silver screen diva Sophia Loren did a famously sensual, erotic, and tantalizing (but pretty tame by today's standards) striptease for Italian heartthrob Marcello Mastroianni in the 1964 film by Vittorio De Sica *Yesterday, Today and Tomorrow* (*Ieri, Oggi, Domani*). The vision of her slowly rolling down her stockings before throwing them at Marcello became so iconic that American director Robert Altman asked the duo to repeat the scene thirty years later for his 1994 film *Prêt-à-Porter* (*Ready to Wear*). *Yesterday, Today and Tomorrow* won the Oscar for Best Foreign Language Film, while Sophia's repeat performance three decades later earned her a Golden Globe nomination. You could always try to emulate her performance in the privacy of your own home.

KISS HELLO, KISS GOODBYE

One of the classic gestures you'll see countless times a day in Italy is the famous "double kiss," *un bacio su una guancia e poi l'altra* (a kiss on one cheek and then the other). Italians practice it everywhere, from the

North to the South, on the streets, in bars, at meetings, during political conferences, in hospitals, at church, during rock concerts—there's not a single place in Italian life that is exempt from this form of greeting. It's practiced by the old and the young, men-on-men, women-on-women, women and men—everybody does it! That is because the double kiss is the commonly accepted salutation for people who know each other, even those who only have a passing acquaintance. It's the equivalent of the handshake or the slap on the shoulder between friends in the States. In some Italian regions you may come across the triple kiss, but double-kissing is more the norm.

As their cheeks meet—as you have probably already gathered, Italians don't go in for the prissy air-kissing thing, they like the physical flesh-on-flesh contact—they'll usually be saying *"Ciao, come stai?"* ("Hi, how you doing?"). If you want to start adopting this habit, proceed with caution. Start with family and close friends first, who may, nevertheless, be taken aback by your new more intimate form of greeting. You should always judge the specific circumstances carefully before you launch into your double kiss.

Since Italians are very sociable, they love meeting up with friends, often in large groups. When you arrive, they will expect that you greet everyone present, so you can often spend a good ten minutes or so on your hellos, giving everyone a double kiss. But that's not the end of it, because the whole process is repeated on leaving, when the double kiss is used as a goodbye, along with phrases such as *bello vederti* (it was great to see you).

DID YOU KNOW ?

Many American women fantasize about capturing the heart of a passionate, hot-blooded Italian male who knows how to answer their every need with an effortless flick of the wrist. But beware, many Italian men have justly deserved reputations as *donnaioli*, or womanizers, playboys who will shower you with compliments, be highly attentive, and add a touch of style and flair to your world, before then moving unceremoniously on to the next woman, such as:

- **Giovanni Giacomo Casanova:** An eighteenth-century Venetian diplomat, adventurer, gambler, author, and criminal, he was best known for being an erotic hero. In spite of being a man of learning, he became legendary for his prowess in seducing women—and men—as recounted in his famous memoirs.

- **Rudolfo (Rudolph) Valentino:** This Italian-born actor set women's hearts a-flutter at a time when the silver screen was still in its infancy. He died at the age of thirty-one and legend has it that thousands of women lined the streets for his funeral, with some even reported to have committed suicide.

- **Marcello Mastroianni:** He carried over his on-screen image as a "Latin Lover" into real life, conducting high profile affairs during his marriage of over forty years to his wife, Flora. He would reportedly even cry on Flora's shoulder on the rare occasions when a woman rejected him. Both his wife and his long-time lover, actress Catherine Deneuve (with whom he had a daughter), were at Marcello's bedside when he died in 1996.

- **(Giovanni) Gianni Agnelli:** Before becoming one of Europe's leading industrialists and head of his family's Fiat car empire in the 1960s, Gianni Agnelli lived the life of a millionaire playboy. Even when he became more of a patriarch figure married to a princess, he didn't make any secret of his love affairs with socialites and starlets, making him a "true symbol" of Italian manhood.

- **Lapo Elkann:** The grandson of the above-mentioned Gianni Agnelli, Lapo Elkann seems to have inherited a healthy dash of his *nonno's* playboy proclivities and could be considered a "new generation" of playboy, with his high profile on the international fashion and jet-setting scenes, and the launch of his own clothing line.

Which Side Do You Start On?

When you start to hang out in circles where double-kissing is the custom, there is the vexing question of which side do you start from—the right or the left? And who's left or right are we talking about? There does not seem to be a hard-and-fast rule, which can lead to awkward bumped noses as you both head for the same cheek. Many Italians claim the kisser always leans to their right first, meaning you go to kiss the other person's left cheek, but that does not always happen in practice. If in doubt, follow the lead of the person you're greeting, which is particularly important if you wear glasses, as a wrong move can even be painful.

YOUR *PARADISO*

VENICE

It is a truly unique experience when the hidden charm of the city, affectionately known as *La Serenissima*, dawns on you after a while, and you realize that the usual cacophony of traffic is replaced with the soothing sound of lapping water. Riding on a gondola may be everyone's dream, but it's not in everyone's price bracket. You can take a less romantic but more practical *vaporetto* (water bus) instead, where there are also a very few open-air seats provided. But beware, you (and your camera) may be splashed with water. Work out routes traveling the less well-known canals, or going out to some of the lagoon's smaller islands (like the glass-blowing center on Murano or the world famous Lido, where the Venice Film Festival is held at the end of August). Move off the general tourist trail and roam down delightful little streets and over charming bridges.

The Double Kiss at Work

If you're conducing business in Italy, or with an Italian, you should still start with a handshake before moving on to the double kiss (it's definitely not a good idea to initiate the double kiss with American colleagues!). It may have been okay for Italian and American presidents Berlusconi and Obama to double kiss in greeting at a G8 summit in the Italian earthquake-ravaged town of L'Aquila, but your boss may not take the same view if you double kiss them at work!

DID YOU KNOW ?

Italy is not the only nation to use the double kiss as a greeting. The French do it too, though their version tends to be less passionate than their hot-blooded Mediterranean cousins'. The origins of the double kiss are not really known, but it could be a throwback to the New Testament, when Judas famously kissed Jesus once before betraying him, thus bestowing the single kiss with the negative label as a kiss of treachery.

In a more formal *lavorativo* (work) context, the internationally conventional *stretta di mano* (handshake) is the more commonly accepted form of greeting, especially the first time you meet someone. But if you then become friends, the handshake is soon replaced by *due bacetti sulle guance* (two little kisses on the cheeks), which is sometimes accompanied by a handshake or by holding the other person by the shoulders, arms, or elbows. You should always adopt the more formal handshake when greeting coworkers who are older than you, though it does depend on the closeness of your relationship. If in doubt, start with a handshake (*stretta di mano*) and then follow the lead from the person you're greeting: if you see him or her continuing to lean in further toward you, you know a double kiss is on the way and you can follow suit.

SIGNING

To the untrained eye, Italians seem to gesticulate wildly, using a flurry of apparently meaningless movements, but these gestures are often part of a kind of second "language of signs" that flows along with the spoken word. *Gli italiani parlano con la bocca e con le mani* (Italians talk with their mouths and with their hands). It's fun to watch and can be a great help if you don't speak Italian, because you can study their hand movements to help you interpret the conversation. This signing also involves a fair amount of touching one part of the body against another.

Why do Italians gesticulate so much? It could be the result of historical happenstance. Over the millennia, Italy has been invaded by hoards of foreign marauders: *Greci* (Greeks), *Turchi* (Turks), *Berberi* (Berbers), *Spagnoli* (Spaniards), *Normanni* (Normans), *Francesi* (the French), *Austriaci* (Austrians), and *Tedeschi* (Germans) have all made claims to the country over the centuries. This history of invasion obviously created communication problems for Italy's indigenous population. If you have ever tried to communicate with someone whose language you don't speak, you probably used a lot of hand gestures to try to make yourself understood. Italians used this method as well, and this second "sign language" has become intertwined with the spoken word as an integral part of communication.

In America, the majority of hand gestures tend to be used as insults, like the classic middle finger. While Italy also has its own set of abusive gestures, a lot of hand movements you see are for everyday phrases, not insults. It is also a great way to communicate with someone you can't physically talk to, whether they are across a crowded room, on the other side of a *piazza*, or sitting in a neighboring car. The following Italian hand signals can create a secret, nonverbal line of communication.

YOUR *PARADISO*

ROME

Crammed full with ancient monuments, world-class museums, wonderful art, beautiful buildings, magnificent churches, and stunning views, the Eternal City has plenty for everyone. When your brain goes into beauty overload, have a picnic in one of the city's many parks. Go for a walk along *il Tevere* (the River Tiber) for a different perspective of the city. Have a drink on the panoramic *Gianicolo* (Janiculum) hill and listen for the Roman women calling to their husbands and lovers locked up in the prison below. And don't forget the tradition of throwing a coin in the Trevi Fountain (with your back facing the fountain, thrown from your right hand over your left shoulder) to ensure your return to Rome.

A dopo: Later (as in "see you later," "I'll call you later," etc.)

Extend the index finger of your right hand into the air in front of you, just above the level of your eyeline. Move it downwards away from you and then upwards towards you drawing a circle in the air (so the circle is not facing you but perpendicular to you.) Repeat this circular motion a couple of times, to represent the hands of a clock moving forward.

Vuoi un caffè?: **Want a coffee?**

Touch your index and middle fingers together with your thumb (as though holding the handle of a cup). Stick your little finger out a little and then tilt your wrist a couple of times, so it looks like you're drinking an imaginary cup of coffee.

Due spaghi?: **(Do you want) some pasta?**

Extend your index and middle finger of your right hand. Curl the rest of your fingers into your palm and put your thumb on top of them, so you have two fingers sticking out, looking something like a rather rudimentary fork. Gyrate your wrist back and forth, as though you were winding spaghetti around your "finger fork." This can also mean the more generic, "Do you want something to eat?"

Andiamo!: **Let's go!**

Bend your right wrist so your palm is facing your body and lay your fingers and thumb together. Move your wrist so your hand moves towards your body. Repeat a couple of times.

Ma che dici! / *Ma di che!*: What on earth are you saying? / Yeah, right!

Cup the fingers and thumb of your right hand together so all your fingertips are touching. Your palm should be facing your body. Move your wrist or even your whole arm in an up-and-down motion. For extra emphasis you can use this gesture with both hands at the same time. This gesture can also mean *Che cosa vuoi?* (What do you want?)

Non c'è niente!: There's nothing left (or "no joy"; for example when looking for parking)

Extend your index finger and thumb so they are at right angles to each other. Tuck the rest of your fingers into your palm. Then shake your wrist from side to side.

Farsi un culo così! To bust your ass! (work hard on something)

Using both hands, position each thumb and index finger to form a C shape (obviously, the one formed by your right hand will look like an inverted C). Hold your hands like this in front of you at chest level (the wider your hands are apart, the harder the task has been) and then move both arms up and down a couple of times. You may come across a slight variation on this used for another rather vulgar expression, *Che palle!*, which translates as something like "how boring" or "what a pain in the ass!"

DATING, ITALIAN STYLE

Touch is an important part of dating in Italy. For example, if an Italian man is taking you out on a first date, he may greet you by **kissing your hand** and then gently **guide you to his car by the hand**, escorting you through open doors by lightly **placing his arm around your shoulders** or on the small of your back. During the date, he may **gently flick the hair from your eyes, caress the back of your hand** or your forearm while he is talking to you, and then move on to **stroke your cheek** and **cup your face in his hand**, usually a prelude to that first kiss. These gestures are not considered explicitly sexual and usually don't come with any "strings attached." They are merely a means of communicating affection, desire, or even passion through touch.

DID YOU KNOW ?

If the Italians excel at courtship and are even pretty good at *fare l'amore* (lovemaking), they could certainly improve on their skills in the next phase of a relationship. It is not uncommon for an Italian man who has showered you with attention for weeks or months to then *sparisci* (disappear) in a puff after they have finally bedded you. This can be an especially harsh letdown as by that time you've probably grown accustomed to all the flattery and caressing. If you want something more than a holiday romance or a quick indulgence, then you should be prepared for the occasional disappointment.

Encourage your partner to feel free to touch you in this kind of way. If he expresses reservations, you can always show him how it's done, and once he experiences how electrifying it can be to feel your skin brushing against his, even in a non-overtly sexual way, he's sure to follow suit and do the same to you.

Common Lovers' Touches in Italy

Here are some of the most common gestures used by lovers in Italy to show their affection. You can easily introduce these simple things into your relationship to generate sparks in your love life.

- Walk hand-in-hand
- Link arms
- Throw your arms around his shoulders or waist
- Hold your hand on the small of his back
- Stroke his arms
- Caress his palms with your fingertips
- Fondle his hair
- Nuzzle his neck
- Touch his cheek or face
- Trace his lips with your finger

Chivalry

Galanteria (gallantry or courteousness) comes as *secondo natura* (second nature) to Italian men. Yes, their clichéd reputation for being

Latin Lovers or Italian Stallions still holds, but in the end it is not necessarily their prowess in the sack that attracts women, it's the way they court you to get you there in the first place. Even if you don't have an Italian man to shower you with attention, you can encourage your partner to add a few Italian touches to his courtship rituals. Typical acts of *galanteria* used by Italian men include:

- Opening doors for a woman
- Kissing her hand
- Helping her on/off with her coat
- Pouring her drink (and ensuring her glass is always filled before she notices it is empty)
- Buying her flowers
- Giving her gifts
- Paying for her
- Calling her regularly
- Cooking her dinner
- Anticipating her desires
- Paying attention to her needs

As the list reveals, Italian men still practice all those old-fashioned courtesies that have all but disappeared in other countries with the advent of feminism and women's liberation.

Tuning Your Radar to Touch-Sensitive

Italian men are always on the lookout for opportunities with women and they exude a confidence and have a *sfrontatezza* (nerve) that helps them quickly move from being an observer to coming into physical contact with a woman. A well-dressed, self-assured, good-looking woman may try to ignore catcalls or comments from men on the street, but she could be passing up on prime openings for a date.

DID YOU KNOW ?

Italians (of both sexes) can sometimes go too far in their passion and not realize quite how hard they are biting! Believe it or not, *morsetti* (teeth marks) are actually quite a common complaint. If you find yourself on the receiving end of one of these Italian hickies, you can always say "*Basta! Fa male!*" ("Stop! It hurts!"). If it's too late, try using some Arnica herbal cream as a quick way to reduce any unsightly bruises.

When Italian men go to a bar, once they've ordered their drink, they'll check out who else is around. If they catch the eye of a woman they like, they will not be shy in coming forward and, even within a matter of minutes, the touching game may begin. Men of other nationalities are apt to stay together, bunched up in a huddle, unaware of everyone else, maybe too shy or embarrassed or frightened to even verbally approach a woman, until the end of the night when the beer has loosened their inhibitions. Ratchet up your awareness of the people around you. For example, notice when someone deliberately makes body contact when brushing past you, and you will see the latent opportunities for love all around.

Pietro Says

La nostra galanteria è proverbiale (Our courteousness towards women is notorious). It is the *arma* (the weapon) that Italian men use to *conquistare* (conquer or seduce) a woman. On the whole, Italian men take pride in being *gentiluomini* (gentlemen). In many other countries elaborate courtship rituals have been cast aside, now often giving way to the extremely direct *"Me la dai?"* ("Will you sleep with me?"). In Italy, however, *è tutto un balletto* (it's all a dance). An Italian woman says *"forse"* ("maybe") or *"chi lo sa?"* ("who knows?") instead of giving a straight yes or no. A direct answer would lead to an immediate resolution to the question, which is the *contrario* (the opposite) of *fare la corte* (courting a woman). Italian women and men are addicted to *corteggiamento* (courtship rituals).

ST(R)OKING PASSION

When it comes to *sesso* (sex), there's no doubt that Italians love it, maybe more than any other nationality. Like many (most?) men around the world, Italians will jump at the chance to go to bed with someone whenever the opportunity arises. The difference is that Italian men will work hard to increase the chances that the opportunity *does* arise. They are also more willing to patiently build up desire through touch.

Italians have perfected the slow approach toward the bedroom—not because they are shy or apprehensive, but because the buildup to sex is a game that they savor and prolong to enhance desire. They love foreplay; Italian couples sometimes *pomiciano* (kiss and caress) each other for hours on end. In other countries, once a couple has become exclusive, long kissing sessions often fall by the wayside. When was the last time you and your partner indulged in a long, lingering smooch? Take a page out of the Italians' book and reintroduce some passionate petting into your love life.

Passione (passion) is of course a key ingredient in sex, Italian-style. Since lovemaking usually comes after two people have been dating, the flames of desire have usually been well fanned. So how can you imitate the Italians' approach to sex? Use these three key ingredients!

1. Massage

Massage is one of the ways Italians use touch to stoke passion. You don't have to be a professional masseuse to give a pleasurable, stimulating rubdown, though it might be fun to take a quick course to learn how to use this touching technique. It's important to create a relaxing environment for your massage, with subdued lighting or candlelight, soothing music, perfumed oils, and a comfortable place to lie. If you have little experience, just imagine what you would like done to you, as your partner is almost sure to like it too.

DID YOU KNOW ?

It's amazing what lengths Italian men are willing to go to to court women. They shower women with all forms of attention: phone calls, text messages, gifts, flowers, dinner dates—both cooked by him or in restaurants, asking you for a quick coffee or drink, invitations to parties, or even just to go out for a stroll. And when you are with them, you feel as though you are at the center of their world; they will *accarezzare* (stroke) your cheek, or brush the hair out of your eyes, gestures that can surprise you with their tenderness. You can feel their rapt concentration on what you are saying, though in your heart you know that most of this courtship is done with one single aim in mind: to get you into bed. However, Italian men are willing to take things slowly to stoke the flames of desire. They can be extremely persistent (in a positive sense) and will not give up the chase after an initial knockback.

Once you've set the scene, gather together some massage oils. Many Mediterranean oils are wonderful for a sensual massage. Try some of these ideas:

- **Satureja Montana** (commonly known as Winter Savory; *Santoreggia* in Italian), which is thought to be a stimulant for both him and her. Since it can easily irritate the skin, don't make up your own massage oil using this ingredient—buy it from a professional source.
- If you want to make up your own soothing mix, try **Melissa**, **chamomile**, and **lavender**.
- Another nice Italian combination is **thyme**, **lavender**, and **rosemary**.
- You can also use **sage**, a potent energizer that's great at reactivating blood circulation. (Its effect on blood circulation means that people with high blood pressure should avoid it. If in doubt, check it out with your doctor first.)

DID YOU KNOW ?

Italy has given the world some of its most famous lovers and experts at wooing. The Italians are famous for being *poeti, navigatori, e sognatori* (poets, navigators, and dreamers). Their passionate love stories have set other people dreaming too. Take these three famous loving couples for example:

- **Romeo and Juliet:** The story of these star-crossed lovers immortalized by Shakespeare was based on two real-life Italian sweethearts from Verona, who died for each other at the start of the fourteenth century.
- **Paolo and Francesca:** Renaissance poet Dante Alighieri wrote of another doomed couple, Paolo and Francesca, in *La Divina Commedia*. Fated to swirl in the whirlwinds of hell together for eternity after committing adultery, their story was also based on a real affair.
- **Garibaldi and Anita:** The man who helped to unify Italy in the nineteenth century, dubbed the "Hero of Two Worlds," had his own heroine, Anita, with whom he is said to have fallen in love after spying her through his eyeglass off the shores of Brazil. She became his lover, wife, and revolutionary companion-in-arms.

You can also find small, inexpensive gadgets for massaging feet or shoulders. Next, follow these steps for a romantic, passionate, and intimate Italian-style massage:

1. Make sure the room is warm enough for your partner to lie naked without catching cold. You can even slightly warm

the massage oil, though check its temperature before applying to the skin—a burn isn't the best start to a sensual evening of pleasure. It also feels nice if you cover parts of your partner's body you're not massaging with warm fluffy towels.

2. Be subtle; don't just head straight for your lover's *zone intime* (intimate areas)—in fact, the most sensual kind of massage can leave these out entirely.

3. Use all areas of your hands (wrists, knuckles, fingertips, and the side of your hand), but don't forget you can use other parts of your body too.

4. Alternate applying different pressures, varying a firm touch with delicate caresses. You can even brush a feather (*piuma*) along their skin, sweep your hair over their body, or dribble droplets from an ice-cube to send shivers up their spine (and not just because of the cold).

There are endless variations on a sensual massage, so customize yours as you like.

2. Focus on Fabrics

Treat your bedroom like a sanctuary. Make it a tactile heaven by decorating it with plenty of soft fabrics. If buying silk sheets is beyond your budget, why not invest in some cushion covers in touchy-feely fabrics like silk, velvet, or lace? Also, be sure that both of you are wearing lingerie in sexy, sensual fabrics!

Pietro Says

In a way, sex is like *dolce* (dessert) for Italians. In Italy, sitting down for a meal means you have an *antipasto* (starter), a *primo* (first course), a *secondo* (main course), a *contorno* (side vegetables), and then you have the *dolce*. Dessert on its own just doesn't make much sense. All the courtship and the buildup to having sex are like these different courses to whet your appetite: saving the best until last. Then again, there is also something to be said for indulging your sweet tooth every now and again!

3. Take Your Time

In Italy, sex is not seen as something you are "obligated to do" after a date. Rather than being a duty (*dovere*), it is considered pure pleasure (*piacere*), an intimate experience partners should relish and remember. It's about *allegria* (fun), laughter, and joy—which are difficult to achieve if one of you is uptight, uncomfortable, or just going through the motions.

LIVE *LA BELLA VITA*
Find a Makeout Spot

Given that a considerably large proportion of Italian twenty- and thirtysomethings still live with their parents, they have developed very inventive ways to find some privacy with their *ragazza o ragazzo* (girlfriend or boyfriend). Some head off to a family house in the mountains or at the beach; others use the *macchina* (car) to make out; and others have scouted out their local lovers' lanes and hidden picturesque spots where they can take their *innamorato* (sweetheart). Scenic tourist zones are often dotted with Italian couples courting, totally engrossed in each other and oblivious to the foreigners milling around them. Even if you have great foreplay at home, change your perspective and scout out a picturesque outdoor location to bring a breath of fresh air to your love life. Don't get too carried away, though—be careful to remain in the bounds of public decency!

An Italian man is likely to be anxious to make sure the woman he's with is enjoying herself. It's not just about instant gratification for him. (Perhaps this is because men are keen to maintain their reputation as expert lovers.) Whatever the reason, sex is a shared bliss that Italians mutually enjoy—try to adopt this attitude in your own love life.

LIVE *LA BELLA VITA*
Splurge on Lingerie

Italians often buy their lovers sexy underwear. Why not follow their lead? For women, choose items in *seta* (silk) or *pizzo*
(lace), such as matching bra and panties sets in *nero classico*
(classic black) or *rosso fuoco* (flaming red) with intricate designs. If this is too over the top for your personality, it's okay
to choose something simpler. The trick is to make sure you
like the touch of the fabric against your skin. Go shopping with
your partner to choose something you both like, attractive to
the eye and for the touch.

READY FOR TOUCH OFF

Now that you know how much touch is involved in everyday Italian life,
you need to be sure your skin is ready for all that attention. Is it smooth
and soft to the touch? Italians assume people will make physical contact
at any moment, and they know preparation is key. Follow their example
by keeping your skin in shape. Try these ideas:

1. Exfoliate regularly when you shower. Use a special mitt, a loo-
    fah, or bath gloves coated with your normal soap or shower gel;
    or alternatively, you can buy scrubs or creams made especially
    for exfoliating.

2. Use body creams and lotions to keep your skin supple. Everyone has their own preference, but treatments containing cocoa butter and aloe are moisture-rich and give instant hydration. Use your cream liberally—don't skimp on application, especially if you have dry skin.

3. Pay particular attention to your hands as they can become rough and dry quicker than other less-exposed parts of your body.

4. Why not turn your skin hydration routine into a sexy activity to share with your partner? After all, he can help you reach parts of your body that would be difficult—if not impossible—to reach by yourself ...

KEY PHRASES FOR TOUCH

La tua pelle è molto soffice.	Your skin is really soft.
Posso baciarti?	Can I kiss you?
Giù le mani!	Hands off!
Quel uomo ha le mani lunghe.	That man can't keep his hands to himself!
Mi spalmi un po' di crema sul corpo?	Will you rub some cream on me?
Vuoi un massaggio?	Do you want a massage?
Mi piace accarezzarti.	I like caressing you.
Vuoi venire a letto con me?	Do you want to go to bed with me?
Vuoi fare l'amore?	Do you want to make love?
Facciamolo!	Let's do it!

FOUR

THE SCENT OF ATTRACTION

I profumi dell'attrazione

The sense of *olfatto* (smell) often goes hand-in-hand with our other senses—especially taste—to create a particularly heady mix of sensory pleasure. So how do you use your sense of smell to live *la bella vita*? Food, perfumes/colognes, flowers, and herbs all play a part, naturally—but even a ride on the back of a scooter can flood your senses with a delightful array of scents. Here are some ways the Italians incorporate a variety of incredible smells into their everyday lives.

Pietro Says

Cooking aromas send *un messaggio* (a message) that you have been awaiting your lover's return, fondly preparing something delicious to eat together. It is a *segnale sottile* (subtle signal) to your lover that you've been thinking about them and planning a *bel benvenuto a casa* (nice welcome home). What could be more attractive and arousing?

CON CIBO (WITH FOOD)

The Italian kitchen is a major source of alluring aromas. This is a concept that's easy to understand! Just think of the scent of pasta sauce simmering on the stove or the whiff of a rosemary-covered roast (*un arrosto al rosmarino*) in the oven. Indeed, there is an old Italian dialect saying that goes "*Quanne dentre de case lu sughe vòje su la pigne, ngi stà né cagnàre né le tigne*," which basically translates as "A nice smell in the kitchen wards off family arguments," and who can argue with that?

Even simple cherry tomatoes, halved then covered in olive oil, salt, and basil slowly roasting in the oven, can recreate a genuine Mediterranean fragrance in your home—and they're delicious to eat as well, whether on bread, in salads, or added to some good *mozzarella* to make a fresh summertime dish.

DID YOU KNOW ?

Italian cuisine tends to feature healthy amounts of garlic, which is considered by some to have aphrodisiac properties. But how can you avoid the dreaded garlic breath? Try eating fresh parsley before consuming garlic to help neutralize the smell. Alternatively, just make sure that you and your partner both eat garlic; that way you won't notice, and your kisses will also be *più saporiti* (more tasty)! Who cares about everyone else around you?

But beware, there is a fine line between an *attraente* (seductive) smell and one that signals a *bruciato* (burnt) or overcooked dinner. When Italians cook, they employ all their senses. You should use your *occhi* (eyes) to watch to ensure things aren't burning and check the clock for dishes needing timing. Keep your *orecchie* (ears) tuned for sizzling sounds warning that your dish is getting too hot or for the sound of coffee brewing on the stove. Employ *tatto* (touch) to test if something is ripe for eating and rely on *il naso* (the nose) to smell when something is ready. It takes a bit of practice at the beginning, but once your "nasal awareness" has been fine-tuned, it can help avoid some potential disasters.

DID YOU KNOW ?

Many Americans believe Italians use a lot of *origano* (oregano) in their cuisine, but that's not true. It is used very sparingly as its strong aroma can drown out the individual flavors within the dish. A much more commonly used herb is *prezzemolo* (flat-leaved parsley), which is so omnipresent that there is an Italian expression "*essere come il prezzemolo*," which is literally translated as "to be like parsley" and means "to show up everywhere."

As you've probably experienced, some kitchen smells are more appealing than others. The smell of *fritto di pesce* (freshly fried fish) can be pleasant up to a point, but then it undoubtedly loses its evocative seaside appeal when it goes stale and lingers around the house. If you are going to fry something—whether it be fish, meatballs, or vegetables—make sure you have maximum ventilation (open the windows and use the oven's fan) and, if possible, shut the doors to other rooms in the home to prevent odors from spreading. Wash utensils used to cook seafood with a good splash of vinegar, which is great for removing fishy smells. Also, make sure you empty the garbage promptly.

Popular Aromatic Herbs in Italian Food

These herbs are a great addition to many Italian recipes.

Basilico (Basil)

Fresh basil leaves are often combined with tomatoes and *mozzarella* cheese to make a simple but delicious Italian appetizer called *caprese*. In addition, crushed fresh basil provides the base for *pesto* sauce, along with *aglio* (garlic), *olio* (the best quality extra-virgin olive oil you can find), *pinoli* (crushed pine-kernels), and *parmigiano* (Parmesan cheese).

Rosmarino (Rosemary)

Another staple in the Italian kitchen, rosemary is mainly used to flavor meat dishes and roasts. You may also find stems of it scattered on a *focaccia*, a flat bread rather like a pizza, served with a drizzle of high-quality olive oil and a touch of salt as an appetizer or as a substitute for bread.

Salvia (Sage)

A common Italian use for sage is to lightly fry some of its fresh leaves in a little bit of butter to make an easy yet tasty sauce to coat filled pastas such as *ravioli*. As well as being used in savory dishes like omelets, it can also appear as a key ingredient for fragrant sweet cookies.

Alloro (Bay leaves)

Whole bay leaves are used to flavor meat stews and hearty bean soups. They can also be soaked in pure alcohol for forty days with sugar syrup added at the end to make a delicious, refreshing *liquore all'alloro* (bay leaf liqueur) said to greatly help digestion after a meal.

Finocchio (Fennel)

Dried fennel seeds are a pantry staple in Italy, used in many dishes, especially anything fish-related. Some people sprinkle just a very few seeds into their *ragù* (spaghetti meat sauce) to add a distinctive taste.

LIVE *LA BELLA VITA*
Use Geraniums to Keep Mosquitoes Away

Plagued by *le zanzare* (mosquitoes)? Try these popular tried-and-true Italian methods. The mosquito repellent properties of citronella are well known around the world and it is used widely in Italy too. However, some Italians also swear by the power of geraniums to help keep biting insects at bay. Another Italian trick to stop mosquitoes from using your flower vases and trays of stagnant water in your plant saucers as breeding grounds is to add to a couple of copper coins to the container. They act as a deterent to the mosquitoes depositing their larvae.

A CASA (IN THE HOME)

Another way to harness your sense of smell as Italians do is to strategically place strong-smelling plants and herbs throughout your home. Put lavender or rosemary in a location where you will regularly brush past them; for example, near the front door. As you sweep by on your way to work or when guests are taking their coats off, the plants give off a wonderful natural smell and can certainly boost the spirit. Scented candles and oils can also create a harmonious atmosphere and instantly transform your living room into a scented Mediterranean villa. Look for smells that have a strong connection to Italy, such as jasmine, cypress, or pine, plants that are commonly grown throughout the country.

TEN EVOCATIVE ITALIAN FRAGRANCES TO TRY

1. *Limone*—lemon
2. *Arancio*—orange
3. *Fiori d'arancio*—orange blossom
4. *Mandorla*—almond
5. *Ginepro*—juniper
6. *Gelsomino*—jasmine
7. *Magnolia*—magnolia
8. *Cipresso*—cypress
9. *Basilico*—basil
10. *Pino*—pine

IN BREEZES FROM THE BACK OF A SCOOTER

William Wyler's iconic image of Audrey Hepburn and Gregory Peck riding around the Eternal City on the back of a scooter in *Roman Holiday* conjures up fantasies about the wind in your hair and the sun on your back as you whiz past the sights, and it sure inspires daydreams of traveling in the epitome of sophistication and style. But riding around on the back of any bike—whether bicycle, a *motorino* like a *Vespa*, or *moto* (motorbike)—also offers a highly worthwhile olfactory experience. Live like an Italian would—check out car rental places in your area to see if any rent motorbikes or scooters, then reacquaint yourself with your hometown via its smells as you whip through the streets!

Pietro Says

One of the things I love most about glamorous Italian sports cars like the Ferrari or the Lamborghini is the smell they give off as they whoosh past. Yes, these cars are known for their design, their noise, and their exclusivity factor, but the intoxicating power they wield is also in part due to the fumes they give off. Perhaps one of the reasons Formula One motor racing is so popular in Italy is because of the testosterone-fueled atmosphere combined with the heady scent of burning rubber emitted by the cars as they roar past.

In almost any season, but especially in *primavera* (spring) and *estate* (summer), the intoxicating aromas wafting around you can bowl you over as you ride past fields, pine woods, orchards, and gardens. If you are traveling to the seaside by bike, more often than not you can smell the salty water before you see it. And if you travel at night, the scents in the air are even more powerful. So even if you can't totally recreate a ride through the Italian countryside, you can certainly climb onto a bike wherever you are, inhale deeply, and discover the "scent-ual" pleasures offered in your own outdoor environment.

Pure country air is heavenly, of course, but even dotting around a city (Italian or American) on the back of a bike can be a treat for your nose. Yes, you may inhale more than your fair share of traffic fumes, but in exchange Italy can offer you whiffs of ground coffee, the sweet vanilla of baking *cornetti* (croissants), the *forno al legna* (wood-burning pizza oven), incense drifting out of churches, or the scent of freshly-washed clothes flapping on lines strung in the alleyways between houses. And if you weave your way through the narrow cobbled streets of an Italian hilltop town in the winter, the air is filled with the sweet aroma of wood smoke. American olfactory delights include the fragrance of roasting meat wafting from barbecues, freshly baked donuts, spices drifting through your local Chinatown, or the smell of roasted chestnuts floating on the winter air.

NEL ACQUA CALDA (IN HOT WATER)

Italy is a country historically famous for its volcanoes, many of which are dormant now. However, even today, world TV news bulletins show striking images of glowing lava flows from active volcanoes like Etna and Stromboli, off the Sicilian coast. And of course, there is the brooding silence of Vesuvius glowering over Naples, with the nearby city of Pompeii resting as an all-too-stark reminder of the volcano's potentially destructive force. Italy is, in fact, the birthplace of volcanology, the study of volcanoes. But all this volcanic activity has another more pleasurable offshoot in the form of *terme* (thermal springs) and sulfur baths.

Italians hit these baths in droves all year round, even when it's baking hot (going in the evening during the summer months, whereas in the winter, spas are a favorite haunt all day long). People make an outing of it, luxuriating in the warm waters, drinking in the fresh air, lounging around in total relaxation, and enjoying a picnic or a leisurely meal.

Pietro Says

A date at the *terme* is a unique and highly erotic encounter. You strip down to your bathing suits and slide into the relaxing embrace of the hot water spring. Since most naturally occurring spas tend to be found in beautiful locations, take a picnic along to enjoy *al fresco* after your first dip of the day, and don't forget a big blanket so you can lie back and relax in harmony with nature. And if you're visiting an establishment that offers massages, why not give your partner a luxurious and relaxing treat?

Many Italian spas have attached restaurants that serve a rich menu of local delicacies to seduce the palate rather than offering the meager plate of lettuce leaves you may expect to find at a termal center. Spas also often sell their own beauty products, made using local minerals as well as other fresh Italian ingredients such as extra-virgin olive oil, grapefruit, and oranges. These products are great as gifts or for a bit of pure self-indulgence, and can be found on sale overseas or purchased via the Internet.

Popular Italian Spas

Spas can be found in every Italian region, but especially in Campania (in central southern Italy, with Naples as the regional capital) and Tuscany (central north, regional capital Florence). Here are some of the top sites:

1. **Acqui Terme**, in the northwestern region of Piedmont
2. **Lignano**, on the Marano *Laguna* (lagoon) in northeastern Friuli Venezia Giulia
3. **Abano Terme**, near Padova
4. **Tabiano** and **Salsomaggiore**, near **Parma**
5. **Bagno di Romagna**, near Bologna
6. **Montecatini** and **Chianciano**, in Tuscany
7. **Saturnia**, in the Maremma area of Tuscany
8. **Bagni di Tivoli**, just north of Rome
9. **Fiuggi**, a few miles south of Rome
10. **Ischia**, an island off the Naples coast

Many naturally occurring hot water springs in Italy are now owned by private companies that offer specifically designed indoor and outdoor swimming pools, beauty centers, and complexes staffed with trained therapists. Enthusiasts can choose between traditional options such as *fango* (mud treatments), mineral water baths, and vapor inhalation therapies, or go for the latest beauty treatments in the form of facials, hot stone massages, and exfoliating salt rubs. Italy's famed spas are often set in breathtaking surroundings, where you can soak in mosaic-lined baths sunk into huge vaulted halls lined with marble columns, or wallow in outdoor pools surrounded by beautiful verdant countryside views of mountains, olive trees, forests, and streams.

Popular American Spas

If you can't make it to Italy's hot springs, there are plenty of options closer to home. Indeed, according to the thermal springs list for the United States, issued by the National Geophysical Data Center (NGDC), there are no fewer than 1,661 naturally occurring hot springs to be found across North America, though not all of these are suitable for bathing. The majority can be found on the west coast and in neighboring states. The areas with the largest numbers of listed hot springs are:

1. Nevada (312)
2. California (304)

3. Idaho (232)
4. Wyoming (132)
5. Oregon (126)
6. Utah (116)
7. Alaska (108)

You can also find plenty of hot springs in the states of New Mexico, Montana, Arizona, Colorado, and Washington.

LIVE *LA BELLA VITA*
Don't Wear Jewelry to a Hot Spring

Take this piece of advice from Italians: Take off all your jewelry before slipping into a sulfur bath, or you'll find your wonderful silver necklace turned into a dirty black chain when you emerge. It can be restored to its former glory after a bit of scrubbing with a jewelry cleaner, but it's better to avoid the hassle (and the shock for the uninitiated) if you can.

It may be counterintuitive to think of sulfur springs as an alluring place scent-wise, but once you have acclimated to that "rotten egg" smell, they are a haven for physical and sensual pleasure. Floating with your partner in a hot thermal spring is one of nature's most amazing gifts.

Create a Romantic Hot Spa Experience at Home

If indulging in a vacation at a spa won't fit in your budget right now, there are ways you can recreate the rejuvenating aromas of hot springs at home. You can do this by yourself if you like, but it's an especially nice treat with your partner. If you spend the time to recreate a spa-like atmosphere at home and you have a *vasca* (tub), your nose (and your partner) will thank you. What's needed for a luxurious soak for two?

1. Dot the bathroom with scented candles to create a sexy atmosphere—try cinnamon, orange blossom, sandalwood, lavender, or vanilla, as all are said to have aphrodisiac properties.

2. Fill your tub with steaming water and add a liberal sprinkling of special scented bath oils, aromatic bath salts, or fizzing soaps—however, be sure to choose smells to compliment the candles, so you don't create an overpowering concoction.

3. Grab your partner, strip down, slip into the tub, lie back, and let the warm water do the rest. When it's time to get out, why not rub your partner dry with a towel instead of letting them do it themselves?

Top the whole experience off with a sensual massage with scented body oils to keep the mood going. You can either buy readymade sensual massage mixes, or you can combine your own using essential oils diluted in a carrier oil—though make sure you carefully follow the manufacturers' instructions, especially if you or your partner has sensitive skin or health problems. Sexy essential oils you may wish to try out:

- **Bergamot:** calming yet very uplifting
- **Jasmine:** a relaxing, sensual, and romantic oil. Use sparingly, as some people find it very heady.
- **Patchouli:** helps to enhance the sexual experience
- **Rose:** sensual and romantic, though commonly more appealing to women than men
- **Ylang-ylang:** a desirable and calming oil with many romantic virtues. Good mixed with **cinnamon**, or with **frankincense** and **neroli** (also known as **orange blossom**).

IN BLOOM

Fiori (flowers) are always popular gifts, whether for special occasions like Valentine's Day or just as an everyday token of affection. Nonetheless, if you have ever been presented with a bunch of flowers in Italy, you know flowers are no ordinary gift. There is an inordinate number of flower stalls in Italian towns and cities. In Rome there seems to be one on every corner; there are so many that one wonders if there is enough demand to keep them all afloat. When you go to a flower stall, the florist will advise you on the best flower for the occasion, thrusting the nicest smelling stems under your nose for you to sniff, suggesting the right combination of colors, and carefully selecting the best examples to turn into a bouquet.

Here are some popular fragrant flowers commonly used in Italian bouquets—they are also readily available in the United States, so you can find them easily:

- Roses
- Freesias
- Lilies
- Irises
- Geraniums

Flowers are a quintessentially Italian way of showing affection, and it's a gift that's easy to give anywhere in the world. The Italian florist really uses their creativity, craftsmanship, and flair to the fullest when flowers are for a *regalo* (present), creating a stunning bouquet to stimulate both the nose and the eyes.

DIY Italian Bouquets

Here's how to make a bouquet that looks like it was prepared by a florist in *Roma*:

1. Assemble the flowers and greenery into a pretty arrangement.
2. Select a large piece of brightly colored crepe paper or colored netting to wrap the flowers, carefully folding it so each fold opens in the opposite direction to its neighbor. This gives a

pleated effect, which when pulled out creates a beautifully wavy effect around the edges of the bouquet.

3. Carefully place the flowers in their paper jacket, securing with tape or staples.

4. Now add ribbons in a color that contrasts with the wrapping paper. Use different widths if possible, and tie the largest ribbon in a bow around the bunch. Pass some scissors along a thinner ribbon to make it curl up, and place it on the bouquet, fastening it in place with a pretty label, decorative sticker, or colored tape.

LIVE *LA BELLA VITA*
Give Flowers to a Man!

In Italy, buying flowers for your other half is not purely a domain for men—Italian women buy flowers for their men as well. To make the flowers more "masculine," take a cue from Italian women and use paper and ribbons in the colors of your man's favorite sports team. It makes the gift even more personal and intimate.

Dealing with Street Vendors

A less romantic but quicker way of presenting a fresh rose to your lover is to buy one from a *venditore ambulante* (street vendor). These hawkers are so common in Italy you may feel somewhat besieged as you try to enjoy a quiet drink, a cozy meal, or even just a *passeggiata* (stroll). You may also have noticed them in major U.S. cities as well, particularly in touristy areas likely to attract couples. These street vendors' flowers tend to have a less powerful scent, perhaps because they have been kept in chilled freezers. So what is the polite way to say no to a street vendor aggressively thrusting roses under your nose? It's always best to look the vendor right in the eyes and say "*No, grazie*," (or "No, thanks" if you're in the United States, of course!) firmly and decisively, and then return to your conversation. If they persist, you can waggle your right index finger from side to side and add something like "*Non stasera*" ("Not tonight"). If this doesn't do the trick, you can say "*Per favore, lasciaci in pace!*" ("Please, leave us alone!") in a tone of exasperation and hopefully he or she will get the message.

WITH PERFUME

The French don't have all the fun when it comes to perfume. Italy has its own long-established history of producing *profumo* and sweet-smelling potions.

A Brief History of Italian Perfumes

Fragrance was used by the ancient Romans in the form of aromatic waters, perfumes, tablets, and fragrant powders. But the Italian perfume industry really took off in fourteenth-century Venice, thanks to the city's role as a flourishing and prosperous trading center with a ready supply of raw ingredients. Exotic spices, fragrant oils, unguents, and resins were brought to *La Serenissima* (Venice) by merchants and explorers returning from the Orient. By the 1530s there was a flourishing perfume industry in Venice. Here are some famous scents developed by Italians:

- **The classic "Eau de Cologne,"** considered by some to be the world's oldest fragrance in continuous production, is an Italian creation. Nowadays the phrase "eau de cologne" is used as a generic term to signify a scent with a lower concentration of essential oils (as opposed to the more highly concentrated, and thus more expensive, "perfume"). However, the original was a scent first created by Italian Gian Paolo Feminis, under the original name of *Aqua Admirabilis* and was a concoction of bergamot, lemon, orange, lavender, neroli, and rosemary. Feminis moved to the German city of Cologne, leading the French to later rechristen the scent "Eau de Cologne." Today, you can find the original sold under the name *4711*.

- **Borsari's "Violetta di Parma"** (Parma Violet) perfume was created specifically for Marie Louise, Duchess of Parma, Napoleon Bonaparte's second wife. The recipe was a jealously guarded secret until Italian perfumer Lodovico Borsari persuaded Parma's monks to part with their techniques for distilling the violet's essence and he started producing *"Violetta di Parma"* at the end of the 1800s. This perfume has a very simple, delicate smell of violets that make it a timeless scent.

- **Another archetypal Italian perfume is "Acqua di Parma,"** first sold around 1916. It experienced a veritable golden age between the 1930s and 1950s, when it became *the* signature perfume of a glamorous era, worn by movie stars like Audrey Hepburn, Ava Gardner, Lana Turner, Cary Grant, and David Niven. Today, *Acqua di Parma* has made a comeback as a modern classic, associated with stars like Sienna Miller, Sharon Stone, and Sandra Bullock. The unisex scent is like a breath of fresh air, with Mediterranean essences of citrus fruits.

Designer Perfumes

In addition to dedicated Italian perfumers, who also create fragrances tailor-made for the select few—like Florence-based Lorenzo Villoresi, the first Italian to win the prestigious "Prix François Coty" international perfumery award—most of Italy's famous fashion designers produce and sell their own brands of perfume. After Calvin Klein launched his unisex scent CK One, there has been a large growth in fragrances suitable for both him and her, a trend naturally reflected in Italy. Here's a short list of some of the fashion designers who also offer fragrances:

- Armani
- Benetton
- Bulgari
- Dolce & Gabbana
- Fendi

- Gucci
- Laura Biagiotti
- Moschino
- Prada
- Valentino
- Versace

DID YOU KNOW ?

In Italy, only an odd number of roses signals affection! If a man sends roses to a woman, the number of stems should really be *dispari* (an odd number), not pari (an even number). This means the classic romantic gift of a dozen red roses is actually not appropriate in Italy. It's better to give your woman thirteen stems—thirteen is not generally considered an unlucky number in Italy, except when sitting down for dinner. (The number traditionally considered unlucky to Italians is seventeen.) If you don't like the idea of thirteen roses, go for the eleven-stem option. If you are dead set on sending a dozen roses, ask for one of the roses to be in a different color to get around the problem of having an even number of the same stems. When sending a bouquet with different kinds of flowers, you don't have to worry about the count unless you specifically request roses be included, in which case you should make sure your rose count is in odd numbers.

The Italian landscape is a popular inspiration when creating scents. Many companies try to capture the essence of a particular location, such as the Eurocosmesi group and its women's perfume "Venice," or Dolce & Gabbana's "Sicily." Non-Italian companies have followed suit; for example, "Escale à Portofino" by Dior recreates the allure of the exclusive harbor resort in Liguria, or the "Enchanting Elizabeth Arden Mediterranean Perfume," which captures the essence of Capri and Sardinia and was inspired by Catherine Zeta-Jones's love of the region. Bond No. 9 has even created a unisex fragrance inspired by the Little Italy neighborhood in New York City!

YOUR *PARADISO*

NAPLES

Used by many as a base from which to visit Pompeii, Sorrento, and the Amalfi coast, the city itself is also worth a visit, with its eye-catching rabbit-warren effect created by apartment blocks climbing the hills overlooking the bay. Vesuvius looms in the distance in the luscious landscape growing in the fertile soil produced by the volcano. Visit one of the city's fish markets to see an eye-popping array of watery wonders ready to grace Neapolitan tables. Check out the local hot springs for a thermal treat, or find a boat that offers sea trips along the Amalfi coast. Try some Neapolitan coffee (they heat up the cups, so watch out or you'll burn your lips) and surprise yourself with how different a pizza made in Naples tastes.

Using Fragrances Like an Italian Lover

Buying your sweetheart a new perfume is an easy Italian tactic to implement. However, buying a scent or aftershave for someone else can be tough, especially as odors change when worn by different people. What smells nice in the *profumeria* (perfume shop) can cut a jarring note when applied to the skin at home. That's why Italians try to take their partners along when shopping for fragrance. It may spoil the surprise, but at least that way you can test the smell directly on the skin of the recipient and avoid any expensive disappointments. Some shops will give you testers or samples to try at home if you can't bring your partner with you.

One way to avoid the potential pitfalls of buying the "wrong" scent for your partner is to buy a new bottle of his or her favorite scent. Just make sure they don't already have some in stock, as perfume loses its potency over time and can go stale, particularly if not stored in a cool, dry location away from direct sunlight. One safe option is to buy some scented body lotion or soap in the same fragrance as their perfume. Alternatively, make a note of your partner's favorite scent and then ask about scents with similar notes at the perfume counter.

You can also apply perfume like an Italian. Many designer perfume houses recommend you spray the scent into the air a few inches in front of you and then step into the perfumed mist to create a subtle effect. Also remember a perfume that works well in the winter may be too heavy for the summer, so try to vary your scents, and choose a "light" fragrance for the summer. When it's really hot, some people find it more comfortable to use a scented body lotion instead of perfume.

YOUR *PARADISO*

ROMANTIC *THINGS TO DO IN ITALIAN CITIES*

In spite of their chaotic bustle, Italian cities offer endless romantic opportunities to share with your loved one. Here are a few ideas for ways to capture that magic moment:

- Walk around the city center at night to see the monuments lit up (Italy is pretty safe at night in well-lit areas)
- Grab the front seats on an open-topped tour bus for a bird's eye view
- Take a river or canal cruise (yes, in Venice, but also in Rome and even Milan)
- Search out accessible rooftop terraces or high points to marvel at the city's skyline
- Explore meandering, cobbled lanes and hidden squares walking hand-in-hand
- Stroll around a market to admire the beautiful displays of mouth-watering produce
- Visit museums with erotic sculptures and paintings
- Rent a scooter or two bicycles (or even a tandem)

- Search out a bar with a great view to have an *aperitivo* (aperitif) at sunset
- Savor a homemade Italian meal at *la trattoria* where the locals eat
- Indulge in some people watching from a strategically chosen side-walk café

One other romantic Italian gesture you can easily imitate is to spray a little of your perfume on a tissue and put it in your partner's pocket, so he will have an instant fragrant, evocative, and erotic reminder of you to carry with him throughout the day. You can do the same by spraying some of his scent on a part of your clothing.

Pietro Says

I love it when an elegantly dressed woman passes on the street, leaving behind a trail of perfume lingering on the air. A dab of scent is always a fundamental ingredient in creating an overall image, but don't overdo it! Many men like a woman's *odori naturali* (natural smells), which can be drowned out by too much perfume. And don't apply fragrance directly to any place where you want to be kissed—if I wanted a mouthful of perfume, I'd kiss the bottle.

KEY PHRASES FOR SMELL

Com'è profumato questo piatto!	This dish smells really good!
Puoi accendere una candela profumata?	Can you light a scented candle?
Andiamo a fare un giro in bici / moto?	Shall we go for a (motor)bike ride?
Dove sono le terme più vicine?	Where are the nearest thermal baths?
Mi porti alle terme?	Will you take me to the spa?
Vorrei comprare dei fiori profumati per regalarli.	I'd like to buy some scented flowers as a gift.
Quanto sono profumati e colorati questi fiori!	These flowers are so colorful and smell amazing!
Ti piace quest'odore?	Do you like this smell?
Che puzza!	What a stink!
Questo profumo è troppo forte.	This perfume is too strong.
Mi piace il tuo odore.	I like the way you smell.

FIVE

A TASTE FOR LOVE

Il gusto dell'amore

For Italians, the sense of taste is essential to life, second to none of the other senses. It is a core pleasure they enjoy every day. For millennia, Italians have relished the art of cooking, eating, and sharing a table. Food helps reinforce emotional ties, through sharing a love of eating with partners, family, and friends. On the international stage, "Italian style" is synonymous with *cibo* (food). Staple dishes from Italy are featured on menus around the world, and many people learn their first Italian words thanks to food: *pasta, mozzarella, pesto, panini, biscotti, cappuccino,* and *tiramisù* (which means "pick me up" in Italian) are all part of the international culinary vocabulary. Food is a mainstay in any loving Italian relationship.

DID YOU KNOW ?

As you know, the Italians love gestures! So it makes sense that they have a way of signaling *che buono questo cibo!* (this food is delicious!). To imitate the gesture, take your index finger of your right hand, hold it up to your right cheek and then twist your wrist, so the finger moves back and forth in a half circle motion.

ITALIAN COOKING PHILOSOPHIES

The origins of the Italians' love of food probably hark back to the times when they knew extreme hunger and poverty firsthand. As the popular Italian saying goes, *"Francia o Spagna purchè se magna!"* ("Whether it be France or Spain [who rule us] the most important thing is that one eats!"). Since ingredients were often in short supply, the average Italian had to make the best they could from a very limited range of items. In fact, some of the most delicious Italian dishes contain only three or four very basic ingredients. This simplicity is not only refreshing to the palate but also light on the wallet, though you should always ensure you buy the best quality ingredients you can afford to recreate the dish's true Italian flavor.

Italy's reputation as a nation of poets, navigators, and dreamers is also reflected in their attitude toward eating: a plate of good food can make you dream—*stimola i sensi* (it stimulates the senses): sight, smell, touch through texture, and of course, taste. Italian sweethearts spend a large proportion of their shared time indulging in food-related activities, whether it be buying the ingredients for a homemade meal, cooking together at home, or dining out.

They Don't Snack

A healthy appetite has become something looked down upon in many Western countries, but the Italians still consider a big appetite sexy, because it proves that you can enjoy the simple pleasures in life and don't skimp or refuse the delights of physical enjoyment. This doesn't mean you have to overdo it and pig out; on the contrary, the Italian idea of food is to eat in moderation and take the time to truly relish every mouthful, making the pleasure last as long as possible, rather similar to the Italian attitude to lovemaking.

In addition, Italians don't snack on what is commonly referred to as *schifezza* (literally, disgusting stuff, meaning junk food) between meals, which means that when they sit down for dinner they are genuinely hungry and looking forward to eating. And as the saying goes, *la miglior salsa è l'appetito* (hunger makes the best sauce).

DID YOU KNOW ?

Italians have a number of food-related superstitions still going strong today. First, Italians consider it very unlucky to place the salt shaker directly into someone's hand because in the past it was seen as passing on sorrow. Second, Italians never pour wine "backhandedly," twisting your hand backwards to pour the wine. This comes from the times when people murdered their adversaries using poison hidden in their rings. They would pour the wine backhandedly, with their ring directly over the enemy's glass, dropping poison unseen into the cup at the same time as the wine. Third, it is seen as bad luck to cross glasses with other people during a *brindisi* (toast), though it can become very complicated when a large group of people are clinking glasses with one another across a long table! And always remember to look the person directly in the eyes when clinking glasses.

They Cook from Scratch

Even in an age where ready-made convenience meals are becoming commonly used worldwide, traditional home cooking still holds sway in Italy, an activity beloved by families and lovers alike as a key way to spend quality time in each other's company. If you walk down Italian supermarket aisles, you don't see rows and rows of *piatti pronti* (prepared meals); instead, you'll find shelves full of dried pasta and a huge variety of canned tomatoes and the like. People still expect a homemade meal, though obviously every so often you can serve convenience foods. Providing your partner and family with a meal you made yourself is not only giving them something tastier and healthier (at least you know what has gone into it), it also represents a small act of "love on a plate."

In order to truly cook like an Italian, you have to get used to preparing fresh meals from scratch every day. It can be difficult to find the time, but with a little planning, you can cook in bulk when you have the time and freeze the extra for those nights when you get home late.

Given that eating is so important to the Italians, some people wonder why they don't tend to suffer from obesity like many Western nations. The health benefits of the Mediterranean diet are now widely acknowledged; for example, using olive oil instead of butter, drinking wine instead of beer, and eating little meat but plenty of vegetables and legumes. In addition, the fact that so much food is still made fresh at home means people know exactly what they're eating and can easily cut down on their sugar or salt intake if necessary. That's harder to do if you buy prepackaged meals. Serving your family healthy dishes shows that you care for their physical well-being.

Their World Revolves Around Food

Food is one of the major topics of discussion in Italy, as we mentioned in Chapter Two. If you eavesdrop on conversations, whether on the subway or the bus or even at the dinner table, you will discover Italians are always talking about food: what they had for breakfast and what they're going to have for lunch or dinner, where to find the best pizza or *gelato* (ice cream), where they found some special regional salami . . . and on and on. This is a passion you too can develop and share with your loved ones—cultivate a genuine interest in what you eat, how it is prepared, and the history behind it.

Train your palate like the Italians, so you can identify a wider variety of tastes and bring more joy and appreciation to you and your family's mealtimes. It can be fun to try to guess the ingredients in a dish, distinguishing the different flavors flooding your sense of taste, refining your tastebuds so you can spot those secret little additional touches that make a dish a fully sensual experience, rather than something to be shoveled up in the shortest possible time.

They Take It Slow

Another fundamental thing to mention is that the Italians' attitude toward their food is the same as their attitude toward courtship and lovemaking: *c'è un approccio lento* (there's a slow approach). Italian cuisine is known for *la lentezza* (being slow). For example, an authentic Bolognese meat sauce (*ragù*) should simmer on the stove for a good few hours to really bring out all the flavors, while you give it the occasional stir and add more liquid if necessary. Try it; you'll notice the difference. While the idea of taking hours to prepare a meal may not, on the surface, appear to be time well spent, the result will make your family and friends swoon with delight.

DID YOU KNOW ?

When Italians go out for a meal, they eat a satisfying, three-course meal: *antipasto* (appetizer), followed by *primo* (first course, usually *minestra* [soup], *pasta,* or *risotto*), then *secondo* (main course of fish or meat) with a *contorno* (side order of vegetables or potatoes). If they still have room left, they have a *dolce* (dessert) and of course a *caffé* (coffee), perhaps accompanied by a *digestivo* (liqueur) to help digestion. The size of this kind of meal may appear excessive, but it actually contains a good nutritional balance of carbohydrates, protein, fat, and greens, something you can easily recreate when you go out for dinner. Ask for smaller portions so you can select a wider variety of dishes without overdoing the caloric intake. Also, adopt the Italian habit of eating slowly (which also aids digestion), and if the portions are too large, don't feel obliged to finish what's on your plate.

The enjoyment is not only in the cooking; it's also in the eating, and, once again, the Italians take it slowly. They adore eking out time in their schedule for the pleasure of sitting down for a collective meal. Even a simple dinner for two can last several hours. If it's a big gathering of family or friends, the evening can stretch on into the wee hours of the morning.

DID YOU KNOW ?

When Italian lovers go on dinner dates, they are usually long evenings that continue for hours on end, starting with a very leisurely meal followed by a pleasant stroll in the fresh night air. By the end of the evening, which could be well past midnight, you may be starting to feel a bit peckish again. As you would expect, Italian lovers have the perfect answer to this dilemma. They head for an all-night bakery, where bakers work through the dark hours, making *cornetti* (croissants) or *bombe* (donuts) to be delivered to cafés in the morning. Can you think of a more perfect way to round off a date than eating a freshly baked croissant still warm from the oven under a starlit sky with your lover quietly munching next to you? *Che bontà!* (How delicious!)

The idea is that good food, like good wine and good sex, is to be savored *con calma* (calmly), not rushed. This means Italians don't just gulp their food down—they take their time over it, appreciating every mouthful. Not only does this give you the opportunity to really taste the different flavors in the dish, it also helps digestion, and if you eat slower, you are more aware of when you're full. If you eat quickly, your stomach doesn't have time to send your brain the message that it's had enough, so you are inclined to eat more than you actually need, thus expanding your waistline.

Given this Italian penchant for leisurely cooking and dining, it should not come as a surprise to hear that Italy was the birthplace of the "Slow Food Movement," founded in the 1980s to counteract fast food culture, protect the heritage of food tradition and culture, and foster the concept of eco-gastronomy in recognition of the strong connections between "plate and planet." There are Slow Food societies operating all over the world, organizing gastronomic dinners to stimulate your palate, a great alternative to popping out for a burger.

They Buy Quality Ingredients

The secret to all Italian cooking is the quality of the ingredients used. Italians will look high and low for top quality produce, often turning the treasure hunt into a full day outing. They will go far and wide to purchase their favorite olive oil or the perfect *funghi porcini* (porcini mushrooms) for an autumn risotto, or to buy the best quality and best value *vino sciolto* (wine sold by the liter), later swapping hard-won information with friends. Putting in this extra effort does not go to waste.

When you eventually sit down for your meal, your plate will pack a flavor punch, and you'll have the added bonus of the memories of a pleasant day out.

LIVE *LA BELLA VITA*
Onions OR Garlic
Though Italians love both onions and garlic, they rarely use them together—so if you're going to cook like an Italian, make a choice! Apply one of the commonly followed Italian food rules whereby you generally don't use both *cipolla e aglio* (onion and garlic) in the same dish; you choose one or the other.

They Use Food That's in Season
While the rest of the Western world only just now seems to be waking up to the realization that food, especially fruits and vegetables, tastes better when it is in season and has not been flown halfway around the world to reach your plate, the Italians have always known this. As well as making the food you serve tastier, it marks the passing of time over the year, with the added benefit of ensuring your menu has more variety. There is something very special about the anticipation of the first autumn pumpkins, waiting to dust off those recipes for *minestrone di zucca* (pumpkin soup), ravioli filled

with pumpkin and ricotta, or *tortino di patate e zucca* (potato and pumpkin pudding).

Not everyone can indulge in the luxury of growing their own vegetable garden, but even Italians who don't have the space for their own *orto* (vegetable patch) grow their own potted herbs on the windowsill. If you follow their example, you will have a ready supply of fresh basil, rosemary, or sage at your fingertips to add an instant Mediterranean zing to everyday meals.

There are many local *sagre* (feasts) in Italy, during which each village or town shows off its seasonal culinary specialties, from the *sagra dei porcini* (mushroom), to the *cacciatore* (hunters' feast), to events for honey, truffles, or *cinghiale* (wild boar), and those celebrating the nut, apple, or wine harvest. For Italians, *sagre* are an excellent chance to expand culinary horizons and try something new. There are certainly similar events in the United States where you can sample delicious, locally produced, and often fairly cheaply priced seasonal food in the fresh air.

HOW TO COOK LIKE AN ITALIAN

The kitchen is not reserved for *le donne* (women) in Italy. Plenty of men are interested in shopping for the right ingredients as well as preparing meals at home. Italian men think women from other countries, especially America and Britain, don't know how to cook. They may even look down on these women, because they think they are unable to satisfy their partner's basic physical needs without resorting to serving mass-produced meals. Knowing how to *cucinare* (cook)—at least the basics—is considered a very important life skill, and acts as a plus in the dating game. Knowing your partner can cook well signifies your life together has more chance of being filled with daily satisfaction and stimulation. Regardless of who's doing the cooking in your household, here are some ways to be sure you're preparing the food like an Italian would make it.

DID YOU KNOW ?

In the middle of a very heated argument about politics, Italians won't hesitate to interrupt the debate with a *"Senti, senti, prova questo"* ("Listen up, try this") to share a tasty culinary delicacy. Perhaps they'll lovingly pass a piece of special cheese they've brought back from the countryside, or a small slice of bread spread with some delicious paté from another region. When they hand you something to try, they tell you where it comes from and perhaps even give you an abbreviated history, so you learn about it, share in it, and be proud of it, like they are. But the message is, just as food transcends politics, it enhances love—love for food and love for others.

An Italian Pantry

Following is a list of the main cupboard staples you will find in every *cucina italiana* (Italian kitchen). If you have these on hand, you can always rustle up something delicious for dinner. There are two additional special ingredients you'll need to ensure your cooking is imbued with the right Italian spirit: *cucinare con il cuore* (literally, "cook with your heart," but more accurately, "a love for cooking") and a love for those you're cooking for!

- Extra-virgin olive oil for cooking
- Special extra-virgin olive oil for salads and for using as a condiment (not essential if it's too expensive)
- Sunflower/Soya oil for frying
- Cloves of fresh garlic
- Cans of tomatoes
- *Passata di pomodoro* (bottle of pulped tomatoes)
- Coarse sea salt and fine salt
- Packages of dried pasta (in at least two forms, such as long *spaghetti* and short *penne* or *maccheroni*)
- Rice for *risotto*
- Herbs: basil, parsley, *peperoncino* (chili pepper), fennel seeds, sage (*salvia*), and saffron
- White and red cooking wine
- Olives for cooking (usually black)
- Anchovies in oil
- Breadcrumbs
- Parmesan cheese
- Ground coffee for making espresso

The majority of Italian dishes are made using *ricette semplici* (simple recipes) that are *facile da fare* (easy to make). But an Italian dish is more than the sum of its ingredients. Since Italian cuisine is steeped in traditions going back millennia, you're not just eating a dish, *stai mangiando un pezzo di storia* (you're eating a piece of history).

Widen Your Italian Culinary Repertoire

There's a lot more to Italian cooking than the same old spaghetti, meatballs, lasagna, and pizza. There is a huge wealth of cooking that varies widely from region to region, and even from town to town. Every place has its own culinary specialty, which, though it may use almost exactly the same ingredients as a similar dish from a neighboring city, nevertheless tastes completely different. Try out this Italian mindset and treat your family and friends to a gastronomic tour of Italy. It helps break up the monotony that comes from always eating the same food. Your family and friends will be amazed at your creativity and imagination, and will marvel at the richness of true Italian cuisine.

Try a Variation on a Dish You Like

Even some dishes thought to be quintessentially Italian vary greatly from place to place. Take pesto sauce, for example. The classic version known around the world contains fresh basil, garlic, pine nuts, parmesan cheese, and lots of olive oil. But there are other ways to prepare pesto—check out how these other Italian regions make the sauce:

- Go to **Sicily** and you'll find three different types of pesto available: one made using tomatoes and very little basil, another similar kind with the addition of some *ricotta* cheese, and a third that contains tomatoes, capers, eggplant, and raisins, with no basil or parmesan at all!
- *Pesto alla Genovese* (the pesto in the Ligurian capital of **Genoa**, the region said to be the home of the "original" recipe since basil was widely grown in the area) is often served accompanied by potatoes and green beans cooked with the pasta and sprinkled with an extra helping of pine nuts on top (even more delicious when the nuts are slightly toasted).

Even if you don't feel like being too adventurous, you can still make small changes to your normal recipes to whip up a new, flavorsome Italian-style delight for your dinner table.

Check Out Some Non-Pasta Options

We'll discuss pasta soon; clearly, it's what most people think of when they imagine Italian cooking. But don't forget about the huge range of delicious, easy-to-make Italian risottos or soups you can use as an alternative for the spaghetti-jaded palate. Again, each Italian region has its own specialties because many of the ingredients are grown locally, are seasonal, and aren't easy to find elsewhere year round. There are Italian soups for all seasons, whether you opt for winter warmers such as hearty Tuscan bean soup, *la cipollata* (onion soup) from Umbria, the tasty Florentine *pappa al pomodoro* (tomato and bread soup, invented to use up stale bread), or a *pasta e ceci* (chickpea and pasta), or try a refreshing summer starter in the form of a *vellutata di zucchine* (cream of zucchini), a light *minestrone,* or a zingy bowl of tomato and fresh basil soup. Here's a delicious Italian soup recipe to try!

PASTA E FAGIOLI (PASTA AND BEANS)

This dish is relatively easy to make, provides an interesting Italian alternative to your usual pasta menu, and is delicious hot, warm, or even cold the next day. You can easily increase the quantities to make a large pot if you're expecting a big group of friends; you will certainly cut a *bella figura* (good impression).

2 cans of *borlotti* beans (also known as cranberry beans or French horticultural beans). You can use pinto beans as a substitute, but don't use canned beans that come in a preprepared sauce.

1 onion, finely chopped

2 or 3 slices of *guanciale* (Italian cured pork cheek or jowl). If you can't find this, a couple of slices of bacon will do, chopped.

2 tablespoons olive oil

Bay leaf

Sage

A dash of tomato paste

1 stock cube (either meat or vegetable)

2½ cups of small pasta shapes (*ditalini*, very small pasta tubes, are ideal)

Salt

Parmesan cheese for sprinkling (to taste)

Peperoncino (to taste)

1. Heat the olive oil in a pot and fry the onions until they are slightly browned (not too burnt), then add the *guanciale* (bacon) and fry until browned.
2. Stir beans (including the water from their cans) into the already fried ingredients and add the bay leaf, sage, and a dash of tomato paste. Crumble in the stock cube and then cover the mixture with water and bring to boil. Turn down the heat and simmer on a low flame for about 15 to 20 minutes.

3. Add the pasta and some salt (if necessary, add more water if it seems too little) and turn off the heat. Cover the pot and leave for 20 minutes.

4. Serve in soup bowls with crusty bread. Add *peperoncino* and/ or Parmesan cheese to taste.

You can easily make a vegetarian alternative by leaving out the bacon and using vegetable stock. To add even more flavor, if you save the hard crusts from your Parmesan cheese (because in Italy, *non si butta niente!*—nothing goes to waste!), you can add them to the pot at the same time as the beans and take them out just before serving.

LIVE *LA BELLA VITA*
Give the Gift of Food

You don't have to spend a fortune on beautiful gifts for family and friends when you've been away from home. The Italian custom is to buy them some regional culinary delicacy, perhaps a small jar of homemade *marmellata* (jam), local *miele* (honey), a special bottle of wine, unusual spices, or some *biscotti* (cookies) made with ingredients specific to that particular location. It is also common in Italy to give special culinary delicacies as Christmas presents.

Think Italian at the Holidays

Just as Thanksgiving wouldn't be Thanksgiving without turkey and cranberry sauce, the Italians have their own traditional foods for specific holidays. Here are a couple of examples:

Christmas

To indulge a sweet tooth at *Natale* (Christmas), Italians serve the now internationally known *panettone*, a large bread-like cake classically containing candied fruit or raisins but now also available in more exotic versions, such as those with chocolate chips. The alternative is *pandoro*, a lighter, more airy cake cooked in an eight-pointed, high-sided pan and dusted with confectioner's sugar. You can buy mass-produced versions of both, but the Italians' obsession with food craft means they search out the best handmade or artisan varieties. Italian lovers always make sure there is a *panettone* or *pandoro* in the house, whether to offer guests or to indulge in a festive midnight feast for two.

Valentine's Day

It is difficult to pin down the precise history behind this traditional day linked to the patron saint of lovers, though it is well known that the month of February has longstanding connections with romance, fertility, and the start of spring, dating back to ancient Roman and early Christian traditions. Nowadays, the *festa degli innamorati* (Valentine's Day) tends to be as commercialized in Italy as it is elsewhere in the world, though Italians are not big on sending valentines (in fact, sending any type of cards—whether for birthdays, Christmas, or any other occasion—is still pretty rare in Italy). They buy classic gifts such as flowers or, even more popular, chocolates such as *Baci*, the popular Italian sweet named after kisses, a message of love in itself. Italian couples also make time to go out to a restaurant for *cena* (dinner) on Valentine's night, perhaps to share a gooey pizza packed with mozzarella cheese, racing to see how fast their lips meet in the middle of the mozzarella string. However, it is also fair to say that many eschew the holiday entirely, claiming *per due innamorati, San Valentino è tutti i giorni* (for two people in love, every day is Valentine's Day).

New Year's Eve

Italians believe that if you eat a plate of lentils after midnight on New Year's Eve, you will have plenty of money coming your way in the coming year (each lentil signifies one coin). Virtually all Italian households prepare a big pot of lentils, sometimes even a couple of days in advance to give the flavors more time to improve. After the ritual midnight *brindisi* (clinking of glasses), Italians then toast to good financial luck by eating a plate heaped with cooked lentils.

KNOW YOUR PASTA

Pasta is such an integral part of Italian life that it deserves its own section. While pasta has now become a familiar dish around the world, this popularity has bred contempt, with the same old recipes trotted out time and again, more often than not served with overcooked pasta. But pasta is sexy! As Italian diva Sophia Loren once put it, "Everything you see I owe to spaghetti!"

YOUR *PARADISO*

CINQUE TERRE

The area known as the *Cinque Terre* (five lands), on the Italian Riviera overlooking the Mediterranean in the North just above La Spezia, gives you a true taste of a bygone age. Monterosso, Vernazza, Corniglia, Manarola, and Riomaggiore are actually five little villages perched on the perilously steep, fertile, and terraced hills covered in grape vines, olive groves, and fruit trees, which drop directly into the sea. These clusters of brightly colored houses hewn into the rocks are really only accessible on foot, by train, or via the water, and are thus protected from modern development. This extremely romantic "no-car zone" seems frozen in time, evoking an era when donkeys and horses were the main means of transport. Many people walk from village to village (it's a total of about five miles), with the *Via dell'Amore*, or Path of Love, from Riomaggiore to Manarola, a particularly popular stretch with couples. Others take the train that stops at each village, or you can combine the two. Make the effort to also visit Portofino just north of the *Cinque Terre*, a pretty little port town popular with the international jet set.

Clearly, Italians are not afraid of carbohydrates! They know there's nothing wrong with consuming them in moderation. This is something Americans haven't quite learned yet. The other key to pasta is that in Italy, it is always served *al dente* ("with a bite," or slightly under cooked), never *scotta* (overcooked). It may seem like a small detail, but overcooking your pasta, even by as little as one minute, can ruin the dish, at least for Italian tastebuds. You must also ensure your pasta is not *sciapa* (insipid, meaning it lacks salt).

Cooking Pasta at Home

So how do you cook the perfect *al dente* pasta? Here are some general rules of thumb to guide you:

- You need a large, tall pot of water, filled with water, although just enough to avoid having it spill over when it boils. The pot must be big enough for the pasta to have room to expand, while still leaving plenty of space for it to swirl around in the water, so it cooks thoroughly and evenly. Measure about one quart of water for every ½ cup of pasta.

- Once the water is boiling, add some coarse sea salt to taste. Don't add the salt any earlier as the water will take longer to boil. Salt can also stain the bottom of steel pans if it is added too early and sits at the bottom before dissolving.

- Only put the pasta in fast boiling water; the cooking time will be affected if you put it in too early, running the risk of overcooking.

- Note the exact time you threw the pasta into the water and then calculate when to start testing it by checking the suggested cooking time on the package.

- Gently stir the pasta every couple of minutes while cooking, to avoid having it stick to the pot.

- As a rule of thumb, fresh pasta only needs two to five minutes cooking time, whereas dried pasta takes between eight to ten minutes, and filled pasta (like *ravioli*, *tortellini*, or *cappelletti*) takes roughly twelve minutes for the filling to be fully cooked through.

- If you are putting small pasta pieces in a soup, make sure the soup is cooked before you throw in the pasta, and also ensure that there is plenty of liquid for the pasta to cook in. Stick to the same recommended cooking time.

- Just before the shortest advised cooking time approaches, taste a piece of pasta to see if it's done. This takes a bit of practice at the beginning, but the pasta should be resistant to your bite, firm but not hard. If it is still too hard, leave it to boil for thirty seconds to a minute, then test again.

- As soon as you are sure it is ready, immediately take the pan off the heat and drain the pasta in a colander.

- Immediately add the sauce and serve. Pasta should be eaten piping hot.

Here are a few tricks to avoid falling into culinary traps and urban myths about how Italians cook and eat pasta:

- Don't add oil to the pasta cooking water. It makes the pasta slippery and unable to "hold" the sauce well.
- Don't cover the pot when cooking pasta.
- Do make sure the salt is properly dissolved before throwing the pasta into the water.
- Do drain the pasta well; it should be moist, not dripping wet.
- Don't rinse the pasta after cooking, unless it is for a cold salad.
- Don't swamp the pasta with too much sauce; you need to be able to taste the pasta as well as the sauce.
- Do add a little of the pasta cooking water to your sauce if it's a little on the dry side.
- Do practice eating your pasta the Italian way, using only a fork. Italians don't use spoons and certainly not knives.

Once you've finished eating your delicious *al dente* pasta, you may find some leftover sauce on your plate. Given that Italians hate to see good food going to waste, before clearing away their dishes they take a piece of bread and make a *scarpetta* (little shoe), using the bread to mop up the leftover sauce. They either eat this little morsel themselves or pop it into their lover's mouth as a sign of their affection and generosity. Please note before adopting this practice:

Italians would not do this on formal occasions or when eating with people they don't know.

Pairing Pasta and Sauce

Italians believe you should use the pasta that's best suited to the sauce, and strange though it may seem, some types of sauces do taste better when used with the "right-shaped" pasta. Fresh pasta is usually made with eggs and packs a greater nutritional punch with a more pronounced flavor. Other ingredients, such as spinach, tomato, or squid ink are frequently added to fresh pasta to give it even more taste. Because fresh pasta is so flavorsome in itself, it is best combined with a delicate coating; for example butter and sage, or a light tomato sauce. The same goes for pasta filled with meat, cheese, mushrooms, or other vegetables.

Dried pasta comes in all shapes and sizes, which can be boiled down to four main types: long strands and ribbons, flat, short, and filled. In general, dried pasta goes well with heavy sauces containing meat or vegetables. Try these combinations for a truly Italian pairing:

- Thicker strands work with a heavier sauce while the thin ribbon varieties are better with a more delicate accompaniment.
- Short pasta is often served with a heavy sauce, which holds nicely in the shape's hollows. Combine short pasta with thick

tomato sauces, or those made with meat, chunky vegetables, or cheese.

- Cream sauces go well with tubular pasta, such as *maccheroni*, *penne*, or the larger *rigatoni*.

- For strand pasta such as the classic *spaghetti* or the thinner *vermicelli*, use lighter variants of tomato, butter, cream, or cheese sauces. However, you can use heavier sauces with ribbon pasta like *fettuccine*, *linguine*, and the widest ribbon of the lot, *pappardelle*.

- If you want to make a fresh, cold salad in the summer, choose short pasta, whether tubular like *penne*, or special shapes like spiraled *fusilli* or *farfalle* (butterfly shaped).

BOOST YOUR SEX DRIVE WITH FOOD

Food has been used as an aphrodisiac to enhance and stimulate the sexual experience since time immemorial, and Italians are naturally in on the game. But because their general approach to food is so sensual to start with, they don't necessarily go overboard on packing their dinner tables with what would be seen as classic aphrodisiac items such as champagne or oysters. Even something as simple as a few fresh basil leaves or a clove of garlic can provide a mild sexual stimulant. They use more common ingredients to turn up the sexual heat.

Italian Alphrodisiacs

Obviously, which aphrodisiac you use and the way you use it very much depends on your tastes and the sexual effect you are trying to achieve: do you want to seduce, boost fertility, reduce sterility, improve potency, or just spice up your sex life? Also bear in mind other important considerations about general health and any potential side effects. Some claim that many foods generally considered to have aphrodisiac qualities are actually mere placeboes, only considered sexy because they are luxurious and pleasurable, rather than having any specific sexual arousal properties. Regardless of *why* they work, try them!

Pietro Says

Italians go crazy for Nutella chocolate spread. While it is traditionally eaten on bread, more imaginative Italian lovers also use it in the bedroom. *Spalmando* (smearing) your lover with chocolate spread, which you then slowly lick off, is a delightfully naughty and erotic pastime for lovers to add to their repertoire. If you're not a fan of chocolate spread, try dribbling some honey over your partner's naked body instead; it is considered to have aphrodisiac qualities.

Here are some favorite Italian foods to put you in the mood:

Acciughe **(anchovies)**	Like many seafoods, these are said to kindle sexual desire.
Aragosta **(lobster)**	Its aphrodisiac qualities are perhaps mainly due to its status as a symbol of luxury.
Asparago **(asparagus)**	A stimulant that certainly owes some of its aphrodisiac fame to its phallic shape, though eating steamed spears undoubtedly makes for a sexy experience.
Basilico **(basil)**	Said to help maintain fertility and sex drive.
Caffè **(coffee)**	Famous as a stimulant, though only use in moderation—too much can turn it into a depressant.
Carne rossa **(red meat)**	Great for boosting your iron levels and hence, your energy.
Cioccolata **(chocolate)**	Increases the levels of the "good mood chemical" serotonin. Combine with red wine for a truly heady mix.
Fichi **(figs)**	Try peeling a fresh fig for your partner and see the reaction as you feed him or her its fleshy treasure with your fingers, Italian-style.
Fragole **(strawberries)**	Popping fresh strawberries into your partner's mouth is a sensual experience in anyone's book.
Peperoncino **(chili)**	A great way to "fire up" your desire, but don't overdo it!
Pinoli **(pine nuts)**	Packed with zinc, these nuts are thought to help tackle impotency and infertility in men.
Rucola **(arugula)**	Commonly considered to have aphrodisiac properties.
Salvia **(sage)**	A potent energizer, it reactivates blood circulation and boosts energy.

Sedano **(celery)**	Its stimulating properties are present in fresh stalks and are even more powerful in the form of crushed seeds to use on salads.
Tartufo **(truffles)**	Their musky scent is said to set sexual sirens ringing.
Vino rosso **(red wine)**	The red variety of wine is thought to be more "chemically" aphrodisiac. Serve alongside some dark chocolate for the perfect stimulating combination.

One word of warning about your sex on a plate: Remember that a heavy meal can put you to sleep; quite the opposite effect of what you are after. A meal that is high in fat, perhaps finished off with a rich creamy dessert and accompanied by too much alcohol may sound delicious, but more often than not, it can act as a wonderful sedative: great if you want a good night's sleep but not the ticket for a wild romp under the covers!

Try this refreshing salad, which uses arugula.

INSALATA DI FINOCCHIO (FENNEL, ORANGE, AND ARUGULA SALAD)

Fennel is popular in Italian cuisine, either used fresh or cooked (for example, in the tasty side dish *finocchio gratinato* [baked fennel], where the fennel is boiled until tender and then cut lengthways, dotted with butter, sprinkled with Parmesan cheese, and then baked in a hot oven until the cheese is golden brown). This particular recipe is for a simple, light, and refreshing salad that provides the perfect accompaniment for rich or spicy foods, or is delicious on its own with just a slice of bread.

2 oranges

1 fennel bulb

4 oz arugula leaves

2 oz black olives

For the dressing:

2 tbsp extra virgin olive oil (the best you have)

1 tbsp balsamic vinegar

1 small garlic clove, crushed

Salt and freshly ground black pepper

1. With a vegetable peeler, remove the rind from the oranges (leaving as much of the pith as possible still attached to the orange), then cut the rind into very thin strips. Cook them in boiling water for a couple of minutes to soften them. Remove the rest of the pith from the oranges and cut them into thin rounds, removing any seeds.
2. Cut the fennel bulb in half lengthways and then thinly slice across the bulb. Combine the oranges and fennel in a serving bowl and then add the arugula and toss well.

3. Mix together the oil, vinegar, and garlic clove plus the seasoning, and then pour over the salad. Toss the salad to coat it with the dressing and leave standing for a few minutes. Just before serving add the olives and the cooled thin strips of orange rind.

You can also try a similar salad that originated in Sicily using fennel, oranges, and spring onions (really just used to garnish), combined with a lemon and olive oil dressing.

Creating a Romantic Atmosphere

Upping the aphrodisiac ante is not just about the food you serve: it's the whole atmosphere you create, so spend time to set the scene with candlelight and soft music before the real fun begins. Eat with your fingers, share food from each other's plates, and feed your partner always looking into their eyes to get their sexual motor running. You could even do blindfolded taste tests to heighten the taste sensation. And if you are planning an aphrodisiac dinner for two, try to eat less before the meal, so that your taste buds are raring to go when you sit down to dinner.

When most nationalities sit down to eat a normal, everyday meal, they are inclined to have *un piatto unico* (a single dish), which they eat to assuage their hunger before returning to what they were doing before. This is not the case for Italians! One meal a day, either *pranzo o cena* (lunch or dinner)—not both—is *dedicato al corteggiamento del cibo* (dedicated to the courtship of food). Italians use the same approach to food as they do to courting their lover. That's why they offer each other great quality food that's meant to be savored.

Approaching Food in a Sexy Italian Way

Italians also pay attention to how a person eats, as they think it signals their attitude to other things in life, especially sex. If you wolf your food down without a moment's thought, it could signal you'll also be rushed in your lovemaking as well. Here are a couple of dos and don'ts for sending out the right messages to your beloved about food:

- **Don't always diet.** If you are always drinking diet sodas or refusing food because you're following a weight loss program, this shows you're *trying* to become skinny. That's not what Italians are about; they *love* their food. Yes, it's good to eat in moderation, but food is a pleasure, and being *permanently* on a diet means you are willing to forgo one of life's delights—not a sexy message.

- **Do eat *gelato* (ice cream) on the street.** Americans tend to buy their ice cream and then hide in their cars to eat it. In Italy, you see people walking down the street with dribbles of *gelato* running down their chin or over their hands, which they then lick off (or get their other half to lick it for them). Isn't that a sexy image?

- **Don't always eat your lunch at your desk.** While there is no denying that work is important, so is your health. If you eat while doing something else, for example working on the computer or even reading or chatting on the phone, your concentration is distracted from what you are eating. Not only can this cause digestive problems, it also subliminally sends out the message that you don't look after yourself properly, which could lead your partner to wonder, "If she can't take care of herself, how on earth can she look after me?"

Romantic Recipes

So, imagine you have a special occasion like an anniversary or Valentine's Day coming up and you want to celebrate with your partner by doing something romantic. What better way than to prepare them a special Italian-style meal, with ingredients to set both your pulses racing? Popular chef and rising star in Italian TV, Alessandro Borghese, has devised a fresh twist on an Italian aphrodisiac menu for two especially for this book. *Buon appetito!*

BRUSCHETTA WITH ZUCCHINI AND FRESH ANCHOVIES
2 slices of Italian bread

1 cup sliced zucchini

2–3 tablespoons extra-virgin olive oil

1 red chili, finely chopped

Grated rind of 1 lemon

6 fresh filleted anchovies

Toast two slices of Italian bread. Lightly sauté the zucchini in some extra virgin olive oil with salt, some finely chopped red chili, and grated lemon rind. Lay the cooked zucchini on the toast and then cover with two or three fresh filleted anchovies per piece. Drizzle with a little more extra virgin olive oil and add a few strands of lemon rind and chopped parsley as garnish.

GIANT RAVIOLI FILLED WITH LOBSTER, TOMATO, AND BASIL

For the ravioli:
2-pound lobster

2 potatoes, boiled

1 tomato, skinned

Handful basil leaves (about 10)

1 clove garlic, crushed

Salt and pepper to taste

2 large lasagna-sized sheets of fresh pasta

For the sauce:

2 cloves garlic, crushed

1 fresh tomato, skinned and chopped

Remaining lobster meat

Handful basil leaves (about 10)

1. Boil a fresh lobster and then remove the meat. Take enough to fill your giant "mono," or single, ravioli and put the rest aside to make a sauce (and a fresh lobster salad on a bed of fresh arugula, if there's enough left over.)

2. Mix the lobster meat with some boiled potato (don't use too much potato, just enough to give some substance to the filling) then add a fresh tomato (skinned and chopped), some torn basil leaves, a little crushed garlic, and some salt and pepper to taste.

3. Take a large sheet of fresh flat pasta and put half the filling in the middle of the upper portion of the pasta sheet, repeating the same in the lower portion, then cover the whole thing with a second sheet, pressing down gently to avoid air pockets. Use a fluted pastry wheel to cut the square shape of your 2 giant raviolis. If the edges do not stick well, moisten with water and press together with a fork. Place the ravioli on a lightly floured surface to dry for at least thirty minutes, turning midway through so both sides can dry out.

4. Meanwhile, make the sauce with virtually the same ingredients as the filling (minus the potato). Lightly fry some crushed garlic in olive oil and then add the fresh tomatoes (skinned and chopped). When they have started to reduce in size, add the lobster meat. Cook for a couple of minutes until all the ingredients have combined. Season to taste and then stir in the basil almost at the end.

5. Cook your ravioli in boiling salted water as usual. They will only need about five minutes. Serve with the sauce, topping with a couple of torn basil leaves for decoration.

CELERY SORBET

3 cups celery juice

3 tablespoons sugar

Juice from 1 lemon

1. Extract three cups of celery juice using a juicer. Heat up one cup of the juice and then add sugar and stir until dissolved.

2. Combine this with the rest of the celery juice then add the lemon juice (and some thinly grated lemon rind if you like). Pour the mixture into an ice cream maker and freeze according to manufacturer's instructions.

TIRAMISÙ FOR LOVERS

As a final flourish, serve this lighter version of a classic tiramisù. It must be *scomposta* (dismantled) so you can feed your sweetheart across the table, spooning large dollops of the heavenly creamy mixture onto liqueur-and-coffee-soaked sponge ladyfingers and into their waiting mouth.

1¼ cups mascarpone cheese

2 tablespoons Barolo Chinato (or other liqueur, such as Marsala, brandy, or even some Tia Maria for a stronger coffee taste)

2 tablespoons confectioners' sugar, sieved

12 sponged ladyfingers

1 cup strong espresso

1. Whisk the mascarpone cheese with the liqueur. Once it is blended, whisk in confectioners' sugar to taste, then refrigerate until needed.
2. Prepare the sponge ladyfingers by dipping each one gently into a mixture of strong coffee (about ½ of the cup) and an extra slug of the liqueur you used in the cream. Only dip on one side, otherwise they will lose their crunch.
3. To serve, put the rest of the espresso in the bottom of a double martini glass (or something similar), then spoon the cream

mixture on top. Serve the fingers alongside the cream, and what you do from there is up to you . . .

ITALIANS AND ALCOHOL

While the Italians love a good glass or two of wine, they have a completely different attitude to alcohol compared to many people in other countries, especially nations like America and Britain. Italians drink in moderation and for the pleasure of the taste of it. They don't go out for the evening with the aim of getting drunk. As you would expect, the Italian drinking culture is an extension of its food culture, which means that they take the time to appreciate alcohol, taking small sips, not chugging in a hurry to order the next round. And if you ask for a drink in Italy, whether it be wine, beer, or hard liquor, if you're not also ordering a meal, the drink will always be accompanied by a small bowl of chips or nuts (often on the house) to help stave off the effects of the alcohol.

There is a cultural reason behind this Italian restraint, beyond the impulse to savor tasty flavors. Up until very recently, Italians considered it an embarrassment to be seen drunk in public. This shame dates back to Roman times and still holds true to some extent today, though the younger generation is starting to lose this sense of moderation. And why was it an embarrassment? Not because you were lurching around and unsteady on your feet, but because it meant you would not be able to perform in the bedroom. Italian males never want anything to impede their performance between the sheets—that'd be a potential disgrace on their masculinity! Something to think about the next time you rush to the bar to buy the night's umpteenth round of drinks . . .

DID YOU KNOW ?

Believe it or not, Italians don't really have a word for "hangover." They don't experience that awful feeling of waking up in the morning hung over from the night before—they would never drink that much. However, now that the younger generation is starting to imitate their international contemporaries' drinking habits, they have started to develop Italian terms for hangovers, though *dopo sbronza* (after drunk) and *postumi di sbornia* (the after-effects of drinking) or the delightful *stato di confusione e malessere* (state of confusion and bodily discomfort) don't quite have the same ring.

In addition, Italian lovers think that flirting is much better and more fun without the effects of alcohol altering your personality and behavior. If you're sober, you can really observe the other person in front of you, pick up the subtle signals they're sending out, and listen to what they're saying, rather than looking at them through "beer goggles." It's not a good sign if you feel you have to be wasted to have a good time with someone.

YOUR *PARADISO*

SARDINIA

This island boasts what is arguably Italy's most beautiful beach, called Chia, south of Cagliari, the Sardinian capital. This vast expanse of pale cream-colored sand with transparent and inviting blue-green waters is an idyllic location for lovers who want to soak up the sun in breathtaking surroundings. Sardinia is also where you'll find the *Costa Smeralda* (the Emerald Coast), dubbed the millionaire's playground. *La Spiaggia del Principe* (the Prince's Beach), a white sandy beach among red granite rocks with crystal blue waters, was apparently a favorite with the Aga Khan, and many VIPs still visit today

For lovers of wrecks and caves, Sardinia has wonderful haunts for divers, providing a hidden world to explore beneath the waves. If you want to get away from it all, the island offers plenty of wild shoreline, untamed wilderness, and rugged mountains to discover. Here the food tends to be rustic, with an emphasis on organic production. As you can imagine, on an island with such wonderful coastlines set in such fertile seas, the range of local seafood is particularly large. Since agriculture, and particularly sheep herding, is so common, you can find a wide range of Sardinian cheeses to suit any palate.

Cocktail Hour

One popular Italian pastime involving drinking is the *aperitivo* (aperitif). It has fast become an established ritual, whether enjoyed as a great way to wind down with your lover, friends, or colleagues after a hard day at work, or as a perfect way to meet up on a date. To give a touch of Italian style to your predinner drinks, choose one of the following favorites in Italy: a glass of *prosecco* (bubbly white wine), a Campari and soda, or, if you want something nonalcoholic, see if you can find the popular Italian sparkling drink called Crodino. Since Italians don't like to drink alcohol without nibbling on something to reduce the effects, the latest fad is to serve finger food along with the *aperitivo*. In fashion-conscious Milan you can find large buffets containing not only the usual nibbles but also cold pasta dishes, dainty sandwiches, small balls of mozzarella, and other mouthwatering stain-resistant delicacies. Italians love making the most of cocktail hours when they're going out to the movies, the theater, or a concert in the early evening. It is easy to adopt this fairly cheap way of staving off your hunger pangs until after the show is over.

Vino (Wine)

Statistics show that Italy produces more than one million different kinds of wines, so there is obviously an option for every palate and budget. A glass of good Italian wine is the perfect accompaniment to a delicious meal. Wine—when drunk in Italian-style moderation—relaxes and helps stimulate the senses. Italian wine lovers are also hands-on when choosing wines—visiting nearby vineyards to taste their product on the premises, and see firsthand where the grapes are grown.

Many lovers who visit Italy make a trip along one of the many *strade del vino* (wine trails) that cross the country to experience the winning combination of tasting delicious wine in the beautiful countryside in the *cantine* (winegrowers' shops) en route. Drinking wine can be an erotic experience as well: look your lover in the eyes as you sip from your glass, or link arms and drink out of each other's glasses, savoring the flavor and building up the sensual atmosphere. Then don't forget to make an Italian-style *brindisi* (toast) before you start, clinking glasses and saying *Cin Cin* (cheers) or *Salute* (good health)!

Pietro Says

Oftentimes in other cultures, you're not having a good time unless you're buzzed. But for the Italians, you're moving into dangerous territory when you feel the buzz. Not just because you could say something you don't mean, and thus create a *brutta figura* (bad impression), but also because when you're buzzed, you cannot concentrate on what your lover is saying, and your performance in the sack will more than likely be impaired. Italians drink very much for the look of drinking and not so much for the feeling.

The Hard Stuff

Italians also drink liquor, though always with restraint. Most bars do not use measures when pouring a drink, so the quantity of alcohol can be much greater than a foreigner may expect. For Italians, the large pour doesn't really matter, as they will usually only have one drink over the whole evening and they don't take advantage of this generosity.

Ten Popular Italian Drinks

Now that you know how Italians approach drinking, why not try some of their favorite drinks? Here is a list to get you started:

1. **Spring water:** Popular brands like San Pellegrino are widely available abroad. Also look for Ferrarelle, a mouthwatering, very lightly-carbonated variety.

2. **Peroni beer:** There are many different Italian beers sold all over the world; deliciously refreshing on a hot day, Peroni is one of the most famous.

3. **Prosecco:** A classic, cheaper alternative to champagne, this sparkling white wine is a perfect start to a romantic evening.

4. **Chianti Classico:** This is probably one of the most popular Italian red wines—it travels well, is generally always of a decent quality, and makes a good accompaniment with many dishes. Barolo and Barbaresco are other well known Italian reds.

5. **Brunello di Montalcino:** Considered by many to be Italy's best wine, this dark, full-bodied, and expensive red is for special occasions.

6. **Pinot Grigio:** Perhaps the best internationally known Italian white wine, this is the perfect beverage for a summer picnic. Other Italian whites include Verdicchio and Soave.

7. **Vino Santo:** A port-like dessert wine, usually served with *cantuccini*, crunchy almond cookies to be "dunked" into the sweet liquid.

8. **Limoncello:** A small, chilled glass of this sweet lemon liqueur is a delicious way to round off a meal. Often made with lemons from the Amalfi coast, there are many varieties available, though it is hard to beat one *fatto in casa* (made at home). Its sugary taste can disguise its potency—drink in moderation.

9. **Grappa:** This spirit with a long history is distilled using the residues of the wine-making process. Today's versions of this "firewater" can also be found with additional flavors, like fruit or herbs. But beware, even a tiny glass of grappa packs a powerful punch.

10. **Amaro:** The name *amaro* means bitter, though there are some sweeter versions of this herbal-tasting after-dinner *digestivo* (digestive). Amaro is considered to have aphrodisiac properties.

IL CAFFÈ (COFFEE)

According to market research, a staggering 14 billion espresso coffees are consumed each year in Italy, with Italians consuming almost nine pounds (four kilograms) of coffee per person annually. The Italians are very persnickety about their *caffè*, and while it is a known stimulant, they drink it because they like it, not purely for the pep effect. Many permutations of the Italian coffee culture have been adopted worldwide, so most Americans are familiar with the *caffè-latte* or the *cappuccino*. But Italians have many other options for their coffee, whether it is *macchiato* ("stained" with a dash of milk), *lungo* (with extra hot water), *americano* (an American coffee, usually from a filter machine, or a very watered-down espresso, served in a larger cup), or even *al vetro* (served in a glass instead of a coffee cup).

YOUR *PARADISO*

RIMINI

If you are looking for a lively spot, you could always head for the Adriatic Riviera, where Italy's clubbing capital Rimini provides powder-soft sandy beaches and water sports during the day, while hip bars and trendy restaurants set the stage for a teeming nightlife. You can dance until dawn in over a hundred trendy venues, with a number of discos set up on the beach in the summer, in addition to the exclusive clubs perched in the surrounding hills.

In Naples (and most of southern Italy), people always serve their coffee with a glass of water on the side. Why? Because large amounts of coffee can dehydrate, so a glass of water afterward offsets this side effect. If you happen to be in Naples and order a senses-slapping cup of their renowned coffee, beware—they heat the cup beforehand, so you can unwittingly burn your mouth on the boiling hot rim of the cup! They do this (either using a special device on their coffee machines or by leaving the cups rim down in a tray of hot water) because a small cup of coffee can very quickly lose its heat if poured into a cold cup. If you want to try this at home, warn your guests first.

In southern Italy, they also often serve a kind of iced-coffee slush, called *granita*, so you can still have your caffeine kick in the 100-degree heat. You can make your own *granita di caffè* by mixing 2 cups of coffee with about ½ cup of sugar in a flat, shallow container. Leave it in the refrigerator for a few hours, then transfer it to the freezer for a few more hours, occasionally taking it out and breaking up the ice crystals with a wooden spoon. If making *granita* seems like too much effort, you can always make some Italian-style cold coffee: brew a pot of espresso (or even more than one to make a good amount), pour into a jar/bottle, add sugar to taste, shake well, and then put it in the fridge to cool. Drink with ice cubes on a hot day.

Making Italian Coffee at Home

There's no better way to give your partner an Italian-style morning wakeup than a steaming cup of strong espresso or frothy *cappuccino* in bed. However, it is difficult to recreate the genuine Italian result at home with an American-style percolator or filter coffee machine. You can buy a fancy espresso machine, complete with professional "frother" attachment, or you can buy a cheaper option commonly found in Italian homes: the stovetop Italian coffee pot. It comes in various sizes, depending on the number of cups you want to make. You just fill the bottom with water, put in the snug-fitting metal filter bowl inside, shake off any excess water, put the ground espresso coffee into the filter, then screw on the top tightly and put it on the stove. It will only take a few minutes for the coffee to come streaming out of the metal column inside the pot and fill the entire thing, usually making those wonderful glugging sounds as it nears the end (a great auditory reminder to switch it off).

YOUR *PARADISO*

FLORENCE

Florence, the cradle of the Renaissance, is a veritable tourist magnet, crammed with wonders to see, and was once home to artistic giants such as Michelangelo and Leonardo da Vinci. This means the main sights can be rather crowded. Walking hand-in-hand over the Ponte Vecchio medieval bridge spanning the River Arno is a must for lovers, then capturing an overview of the city by going into the hills around Fiesole, a town offering breathtaking panoramas over the Florentine rooftops. Sample some of the exquisite regional food, like the famous *bistecca alla fiorentina*, a Florentine style T-bone steak.

If you want some frothy cappuccino-style milk, there are simple, low-cost do-it-yourself frothers on the market. They're basically a small metal jug with a lid, attached with what looks like a very fine sieve on a pole. You just warm the milk up (2 percent milk seems to work the best) until just below the boiling point, and then insert the lid and pull the pole up and down vigorously for a few times until you can feel it's starting to meet resistance. Take off the lid and voilà—frothy milk for a perfect cappuccino in your own home. Your partner will adore you for giving them the perfect start to their morning.

KEY PHRASES FOR TASTE

Il mio piatto preferito sono le fettuccine al ragù.	My favorite dish is fettuccine with meat sauce.
Ti va un piatto di pasta?	Would you like a plate of pasta?
Butta la pasta!	Start cooking the pasta! (literally, throw in the pasta)
Questa mozzarella è squisita!	This mozzarella is absolutely delicious!
Ho una certa fame!	I'm really hungry!
Adoro i dolci.	I love desserts. (I have a sweet tooth.)
Andiamo a cucinare.	Let's go and cook.
Passami il sale.	Pass me the salt.
Facciamo un brindisi!	Let's make a toast!
Andiamo a mangiare fuori stasera?	Shall we eat out tonight?
Facciamo un picnic?	Shall we go on a picnic?
Ti ho portato una scatola di Baci.	I've brought you a box of Baci chocolates.
Stasera ti ho preparato qualcosa di speciale!	I've prepared something special for you tonight!
Ti spalmerei di Nutella per mangiarti tutto/a!	I'd like to cover you in Nutella and eat you all up!
Buon appetito!	Enjoy your meal!

SIX

THE BEAUTIFUL LIFE
La bella vita

People the world over envy the Italians for living the *bella vita* (beautiful life). Italians are, after all, renowned for making the most of every opportunity for pleasure and relaxation. Living *la bella vita* signifies many things—from an appreciation for family and friends to finding beauty in everyday moments. Understanding where this attitude comes from and paying particular attention to all the ways Italians summon up the beautiful life in their everyday world will not only increase the quality time you spend with your loved ones, but it will also generate greater mutual enjoyment and understanding. It is also relatively cheap to achieve, so you can enjoy it in good economic times or bad. So what is it that makes the Italian life so beautiful?

THE IMPORTANCE OF FAMILY

Italians are first and foremost family-oriented, always putting *la famiglia* before anything else. To American eyes this may seem overly sentimental, oppressive, small-minded, or even sappy, but for the Italians, family is the glue that makes individuals feel part of a larger whole.

Family in Italy not only means parents and children but also grandparents, uncles, aunts, and cousins. Italian families regularly go out for a meal as a group, usually for Sunday lunch, with as many as three or four generations sitting around the same table, eating, laughing, and enjoying each other's company. In Italy, you generally won't find Grandma in a nursing home. Instead, she is actively involved in family life, and her wisdom and knowledge (and her cooking!) are lapped up by the younger generations. Having her shoulder to cry on is yet another benefit for Italian families. Italians will look to their elders for advice, even with their love lives.

Italian fathers also understand the importance of family. They make time for their kids, taking them to the soccer game, teaching them how to ride their first *motorino* (scooter), taking them out for ice cream, or playing games such as *biliardino* (table soccer) together. Their relationships with their children are a top priority. But nowhere is the family glue more powerful than in childrens' bonds with Italian mothers.

MAMMA MIA (MOTHER OF MINE)

While the male-dominated business and political spheres in Italy still have plenty of progress to make regarding their treatment of females, women reign supreme in the family and in relationships. *La mamma* (the mother) rules over the home and brings sensitivity and softness to relationships with the family. While they are often portrayed as overbearing, excessively protective, or clingy, the best Italians moms are really a study in contradictions: sexy and nurturing, strong and vulnerable, serious and playful. Think of the characters played by Anna Magnani and Sophia Loren in Italian films and you will have a good idea of the ideal Italian mother figure.

Society respects Italian mothers. If an Italian wants to sit at a nice table in a restaurant, sample some free chocolates, or even access a cordoned-off spot, all she has to say is "*è per la mamma*" ("it's for my mom") and all doors are opened.

Mammoni (Mama's Boys)

Approximately eight out of ten Italians under thirty still live at home, and about 67 percent of them are men. These figures were widely reported in the press in October 2007 after the Italian Finance Secretary Tommaso Padoa-Schioppa floated the idea of government tax-relief measures to help youngsters he controversially dubbed *bamboccioni* (big kids) leave home. Many foreign women say it is difficult to meet an Italian man younger than forty who has left the parental nest. And if they *have* managed to leave home, those apron strings are still not completely severed, as around 43 percent of Italians are reported to rent or buy homes less than a mile from their parents (again, according to Padoa-Schioppa). These men who stay close to their parents obviously strengthen their family ties but also create a source of potential strain, especially when more independent-minded partners come along. Dubbed *mammoni* (mama's boys), these men cite the cost of living (especially rental accommodation) and lack of work prospects as reasons for their protracted presence in the family home. But when pushed, they do admit it is also because it's great to have Mom around to cook her tasty pasta sauce for dinner and do their washing and ironing! The most common excuse these men give for staying put is that they "love their parents." Perhaps overly clingy parents are also to blame, possibly further encouraged by the promise of their child's financial contribution (however small) to the household.

Understanding an Italian Mother-in-Law

Not only do the Italians love their mothers, but Italian moms also coddle their children, particularly the boys, pampering them, tending to their every need, and treating them like royalty. So when a woman hooks up with an Italian man, she often needs to overcome not another mistress or lover, but *la mamma*. If your partner is an Italian man whose mother catered to his every need, you may find yourself struggling to help him understand that you won't do the same thing. Mothers' caretaking rubs off on the kids, who go around thinking they *are* royalty and deserve to be treated as such (admittedly something that can also happen in non-Italian households). On the positive side, this attitude can engender great self-confidence and help children become accepting and trusting of other people. Italian kids are not necessarily expected to be brave and cope with life on their own, which is perhaps why they are also more social when they grow up—they crave companionship of all kinds.

Pietro Says

Loving and having respect for your parents may seem simple, but true respect also means making time for them, eating around the same table as a family, going out with them, and including them in your lives. Italian children do those things. Even a busy man in his sixties like Fabio Capello, the Italian soccer coach who now heads the English national squad, makes daily calls to his mom in Italy. He reportedly tells her that he misses her, and her home cooking!

However, this attitude can also be the source of problems in a relationship, so try to find a middle ground with your partner. You can treat your man well—praise him when appropriate, but try not to pander to his every whim or neuroses. You're not his mother! No one is suggesting you become a carbon copy of your man's mom, especially given that *la mamma è sempre la mamma* (the mother is always the mother, meaning you can't really ever compete with her on equal terms) and she usually represents a difficult, if not impossible figure to live up to. But here's how to make the Italian tradition work for you: customize your own version of these classic and dominant Italian maternal traits that can go a long way to nurture your romance. Yes, on the surface they may sound a bit chauvinistic, but if you have a modern-thinking man, these are things you can share as a team, creating a warm, loving environment that is a real home for both of you:

- Be as good as his mother is in the kitchen.
- Keep a clean, tidy house.
- Raise your children properly.
- Be sympathetic about his problems.
- Take good care of his clothes and yours.
- Let him know you are concerned for him and his welfare.

And don't forget the one weapon in your armory to gently free your man from his doting mother's apron strings, something she can never give him: gratifying sex on a regular basis.

Becoming an Italian Mamma Yourself

How can you become like these well-respected, doting moms? The delicate balance of opposites mentioned on page 177 is a difficult trick to pull off, but it is worth trying not only for yourself, but for your children and husband as well. Here are some pointers:

- Keep your body in good shape by working out.
- Wear clean, figure-hugging clothes, not sloppy sweatsuits stained with baby spit up.
- Maintain a young, fresh look—don't feel you have to look your age (but don't overdo it).
- Practice your video gaming skills so you can give your kids a run for their money.
- Don't go to pieces in front of anyone. Cry in the privacy of your own bathroom, then use a judicious dash of concealer to emulate the perfect composure when you emerge.
- Don't panic or have a meltdown in public; always look like you're holding it together.
- Don't continually whine, moan, or complain—avoid the image of being a "grumpy old woman" by adopting a positive outlook on life's problems.
- Polish your repartee and witty one-liners.
- Smile!

Be a Sexy Mom

Once Italian women become mothers, while they naturally devote themselves to their kids, they do not neglect their personal appearance and still make an effort with their relationship. They know it's still possible to be alluring and sexy, something that is sometimes forgotten in many other countries. They get back in shape after giving birth, they still wear glamorous curve-enhancing clothing with plunging necklines, and they wear makeup and ensure they look their best when going out—things many mothers let fall by the wayside with the pressure of looking after the kids.

Pietro Says

One tack Italian men use when trying to date a woman is to say that he can introduce her to people, and that he has good connections and can put in a word on her behalf. The culture of *raccomandazioni* (recommending people) is prevalent in Italy; it's not necessarily what you know, but who you know that counts here. This system can be frustrating when you want to be considered on your merits alone, but since others are playing this game, you should try to exploit it to your own advantage. This is not to say the importance of fostering contacts and developing a social network doesn't hold true in other countries; it's just the Italians have got it down to a fine, if not sometimes corrupt, art.

See Your Kids as a Pleasure

If your friends and family love children, try to include them in as many activities as possible, like the Italians do. The freedom to take your kids with you virtually everywhere you go, knowing they will not merely be tolerated but warmly accepted (if not venerated), is a wonderful luxury for parents. It reduces any sense of isolation created by staying cooped up at home with the kids, and provides a welcome break, which can certainly help dissipate tensions and resentment that can build up between partners. It also creates an excellent opportunity for some quality family time. Make the most of child-friendly places in your area, and get out with the brood for some fresh air and a new perspective. Leaving the house creates a sense of freedom and space, and is another way Italian lovers ease the pressures of daily life. Now you can, too.

In Italy, children are included in virtually all non-work-related activities, and Italian adults are very flexible (some may say lax) about things like bedtime. View your kids as a fundamental part of every gathering so that you don't have to worry about organizing babysitters or getting home early. If you're going out for dinner, take the children along too, and when they're tired, push a couple of seats together to form a makeshift bed so they can sleep while the evening continues, and carry them home over your shoulders at the end of the night—a sight you will see on any evening in an Italian city. Adopting some of this flexibility, and seeing your kids as a pleasure, not a hindrance or a burden, can have positive spinoffs in your relationship, as you don't feel as tied to the house to watch over the little ones.

NURTURING FRIENDSHIPS

Relationships with friends and even passing acquaintances are vitally important for Italians. Couples always seem to have both friends and family regularly involved in their lives. And the emphasis placed on friendship creates a wonderful atmosphere of solidarity and support. Admittedly, it can be occasionally tiring to have so little time for yourself, but the advantages of being surrounded by people who genuinely care about you far outweigh the negative aspects.

Raccomandazioni (It's Not What You Know But Who You Know)

Having a tight-knit group of good friends can also have other advantages, particularly in the realm of networking. If you and your partner work as an Italian-style team, helping each other out by putting in a good word in the right ears, all the better. Knowing you can rely on a network of close friends to introduce you to people that count or to *raccomandarti* (recommend you) can be a wonderful resource when you need a variety of things—a new job, a good nanny, or an honest mechanic. You can adopt this Italian attitude in your life by readily swapping useful information with your family and friends, sharing it for everyone's benefit, rather than jealously guarding your knowledge and contacts.

BE NICE TO STRANGERS

In Italy, once you have been to a place a couple of times, the people working there tend to recognize you and greet you. For example, if you go to the same coffee shop, after two or three times the barman will say "hi" to you, know how you like your drink or your sandwich, and start to prepare it even before you've placed your order. A passing acquaintance in Italy is more than a passing acquaintance, and this knowledge makes interaction on any level more human and real.

LIVE *LA BELLA VITA*
Welcome New Additions

When an Italian couple has a baby, they hang blue or pink flower-shaped decorations outside their door, according to the custom. This serves to announce the arrival of the little one and to share the joy in the birth of their child with their neighbors and the whole community. Why not duplicate this lovely Italian way of spreading your happy news? Your neighbors may be more willing to offer a helping hand if they feel a part of your family circle.

Why not say hello to your neighbors as you pass them on the stairwell? Try to adopt a more Italian attitude to your fellow human being by casting off that paranoia about other people and assuming a more open and caring attitude. The benefits of this way of thinking are obvious: it is satisfying to be considered as an individual, a human being, and the fact that someone remembers you creates a little glow, makes you feel appreciated, lifts your spirits, and has a positive effect on your general mood. It doesn't take much to make a little effort to pay attention to others, and the rewards for you as a person, for your relationships, and your general standing in the community are manifold.

LIVE *LA BELLA VITA*
Celebrate Onomastico

A perfect example of how people care for others is the *onomastico* (name day), which is almost more important than a birthday in Italy. Many Italian people are named after saints, and your *onomastico* is the day that corresponds to your saint's feast day. Since many passing acquaintances may not know the date of your birthday, this saint's day is an opportunity for them to send you *auguri* (good wishes) in the form of phone calls, messages, and even presents. You can check when your special day falls within the "saint of the day" section on the Roman Catholic Church website run by the Franciscans, *www.americancatholic.org*.

In addition to paying attention to daily casual contacts, Italians actually make time to develop their personal relationships, whether it be grabbing a quick coffee to catch up or organizing weekends away with friends. Everyone knows that making the time to talk and be together can be beneficial for a couple. Since the pace of life in Italy is somewhat slower than it is in America, people are less time-starved and even those with stressful jobs can find a moment to make a quick call to a friend who is down, or send a loving message to their partner. It is these little things that make life beautiful—reminding you that you're not just a rat on a treadmill but a person, surrounded by other people.

TIME FOR *VACANZE*

The Italians consider *vacanze* (a vacation or time off from work) as indispensable to living a good life. The concept of all work and no play is foreign to Italian nature. It doesn't hurt that the Italian calendar is filled with national or local holidays that provide chances for plenty of time off. And, since these holidays often fall on a weekday, the Italians try to make the most of that valued break, even using a couple of days of their annual vacation allowance (very generous by American standards, averaging at around thirty days a year) to cover the period up to the weekend, thus carving out the most vacation time possible. These periods are called *ponti* (bridges), with the idea being that you use a national holiday as a bridge, which hopefully also encompasses the weekend, to have a short but sweet continual block of leisure time with your partner and family.

While many Americans seem almost allergic to taking time off from work (even renouncing the vacation time owed to them), Italians know that slaving away, day after day, for months on end is not only unproductive work-wise and bad for your health, but is also a highly destructive factor in relationships. There is some truth to the old adage "All work and no play makes Jack a dull boy," the Italian equivalent of which is *Il lavoro senza gioia fa della vita una noia* (Work without joy makes life boring).

YOUR *PARADISO*

CAPRI

Italy has plenty of small islands for the perfect lovers' retreat. Near Naples is enchanting Capri (featured in a recent Dolce & Gabbana worldwide TV campaign for a new perfume) and its famous *Grotta Azzura* (Blue Grotto) sea cave. Nearby is the thermal island resort of Ischia and the charming Procida (used as a location for the film *Il Postino*). If you're in search of a taste of "real Italy," sail to the nearby smaller and lesser well-known, but equally picture-perfect Ponza, or search out the hidden treasures to be found on the island of Giglio. One more island worth mentioning is Elba (where Napoleon was exiled) with its *Spiaggia dell'Innamorata* (Lover's Beach). Located off the southeastern promontory of Monte Calamita, the most popular pastime for lovers is to snorkel out to the nearby Gemini islets, to spy on the teeming sea life there.

So take a break. And while you're at it, ditch the cell phone and laptop. Nothing is more demoralizing, disappointing, or even degrading than watching your loved one spend more time answering e-mails and phone calls than being with you when the two of you are on vacation. The Italians know no one is indispensable and that there are immeasurable benefits to taking a proper break, both for your work and for your personal, familial, and emotional relationships.

Another valuable lesson for Americans is the Italian attitude toward work. They work to live, not live to work. This emphasis on *living* as more important than *working* means that they are able to *staccarsi* (cut off) from work when they get home, an obvious benefit for any relationship. This does not mean they don't care about work, it means that a person's job is simply in *secondo piano* (second place) in their lives. The old-school, totally carefree "leave it to tomorrow" attitude of the Italians is on the wane in a globalized world that never sleeps, but they still manage to carve out a better work-life balance, thus reducing the inevitable tensions caused by the rat race. So how do Italians spend all this free time? Here are just a few of the ways they wind down together:

- Exploring other cities
- Walking in the countryside
- Lounging at the beach
- Going on a winter weekend skiing trip
- Staying with friends in their second homes outside of the city
- Inviting friends over for dinner
- Sitting down for a relaxing game of cards with friends
- Going out for a relaxing *aperitivo* (aperitif) in a local open-air bar in a pretty *piazza*
- Locking the door, taking the phone off the hook, and spending the weekend in bed with their partner

Basically, Italians will grab at any opportunity to enjoy the *bel tempo* (nice weather) for which their country is renowned. A change of environment is undoubtedly a great way to relax, kickstart your tired and perhaps jaded outlook on life, and experience different worlds. Getting away for a little while, even just for a couple of days, can help you and your partner step back from the grind of daily life and share something new. Just make sure you leave your BlackBerry at home!

PHILOSOPHIES OF *LA BELLA VITA*

Italy has a wonderful culture, beautiful people, millennia of history, breathtaking landscapes, and incredible art. It is a great country for hanging out and enjoying the abundant pleasures life has to offer. But no matter where you are, you can live like an Italian. Look for opportunities to kick off your shoes, lay back, and contemplate the world around you. Moments of pure, yet simple enjoyment are a real tonic for the soul.

Relax!

Italians embrace the idea that it's good to take time to just chill out; an appointment book crammed with things to do can kill any chance for spontaneity. While you of course need to plan for specific events, leave room for opportunities to do things on the spur of the moment. You don't always have to be packing in loads of events, which can be entertaining, but can also cause strains and add pressure to an already busy life.

Appreciate the simple things in life, the little joys you can find 24/7 if you only look. For example, people watching can be fun if you make up stories about how you imagine their lives to be. If you do this with your partner, you two can even exchange innocent opinions on your physical likes and dislikes, which can help you get to know your partner more intimately (the Italians love to do that!).

Pietro Says

Italians walk! Have you actually looked at the buildings in your neighborhood? Make time to watch the trees and flowers change with the seasons in your local park. Walk without any specific purpose and you will see beautiful things. Take your partner by the hand and go for an Italian-style "aimless" ramble.

Find Simple Joys

One of the keys to enjoying *la bella vita* is to take pleasure in the simple joys you can find around you every day. The slower pace of life in Italy gives people more time to appreciate the world around them, as they are not rushing from place to place in a frantic whirlwind. Beauty is everywhere, and the Italians take the time to note the *bellezza* around them. They will smell a rose, admire a beautiful building, stop to watch the sun set over the hills, notice the changing of the seasons, or appreciate the smile of a stranger on the subway. If you open your eyes to beauty everywhere, it will enrich your life, bringing innocent (and inexpensive) pleasures into your world. When you take time to appreciate life, you fill your existence with tiny joys that bring enormous peace and pleasure. If you leave space for life to "unfold," these small wonders can make even the most mundane moment magical.

YOUR *PARADISO*

THE MOUNTAINS AND LAKES

If you are looking for a romantic getaway in the heart of nature, then Italy comes to the fore yet again, whether you want to go skiing, mountain trekking, or just want to relax and appreciate the landscape's wild beauty. Italy has two main mountain ranges, the Alps and the Apennines. The Alps are in the North, where you will find the famous Dolomites (in the South Tyrol and Trentino regions: the main skiing resorts are here, including the world renowned Cortina). The *Appennini* (the Apennines) are the other range, forming the country's backbone, running more or less north to south. Italy's mountains and lakes provide the perfect location for a delicious picnic *al fresco* in the open air, or a picturesque *aperitivo* watching the sun go down. Hire a boat or a *pedalò* or a canoe for two on the lakes and splash out to the center of the water to commune with nature and enjoy the surrounding silence. If you're the trekking type, check out if there is a *rifugio* (a small mountain shelter) on your route, an ideal hideaway for lovers to cuddle up in front of a log fire in the midst of majestic surroundings.

For a lake holiday, sample the delights offered by the resorts north of Milan, such as Maggiore, Lugano, and of course Como, now home to George Clooney. These idyllic lakes set among high peaks are frequented by the Milanese searching for some peace from the city hubbub, rubbing shoulders with the visiting VIPs and international tourists to create a unique ambience.

Practice the Art of Arrangiarsi

In Italy, one of the prevailing philosophies is that you take what life throws at you and find a way around any problem, known as the art of *arrangiarsi* (fixing things as best you can). Italians excel at thinking outside of the box, using creativity to solve problems. This flexibility can help reduce any stifling feelings of an overly rigid approach to life. Going with the flow is the order of the day, an attitude that can make you more forgiving and less severe or strict if things don't go precisely how you expect in your life.

Let Your Emotions Out!

It is not always easy to confide in your partner, and many people find it hard to truly open up to their lover, because they are afraid of showing their weaknesses, fears, or emotions. In Italy, being emotional is considered a positive, to be encouraged, not frowned upon. *Emozioni* (emotions) of any sort, even negative feelings such as sadness, are lauded as being very human and this applies to men as well as women. Letting out your emotions proves you're not an "ice queen." Sharing your inner turmoil or worries can bring you closer to your partner, giving them a chance to show empathy and give moral support, while clearly illustrating they can do the same with you, something you should encourage—though you should be careful that the emotional venting doesn't become too one-sided. Sharing your troubles can bring greater intimacy, creating a bond between you and your partner, shaped and strengthened in the good times and in the bad. If you don't feel your partner can be there for you, then there is something lacking in your relationship.

When it comes to *felicità* (happiness), the Italians seem to have it figured out. Their priorities are different and they place more emphasis on spending time with their partners, family, and friends, and enjoying the simple pleasures they can afford. Although they are interested in materialistic things up to a point, they are less driven by the idea of wealth and success. Their general feeling is that all they need in life is *un po' di soldi* (a little bit of money) and a *pizzico di fortuna* (smattering of luck). Obviously the American dream entails achieving much more than that, and it propels and even pressurizes people into choices that can sideline other equally important aspects of their lives. Perhaps Italians come across as being very happy because they don't have the materialistic desires Americans have. Living a more simple, pared-down life can have countless benefits.

This is a simple recipe, but one that Italian couples have proved still works even in this modern age with its lack of time and overabundance of loneliness. Even making minor changes to your priorities and your perspective can help you and your other half enjoy *la bella vita*, and to bring out the beauty there just waiting to be enjoyed. Enhancing this elusive "sixth sense," in addition to adopting the Italian approach to the other five physical senses, can stimulate all areas of your life, enabling it to blossom in all its potential glory.

KEY PHRASES FOR *LA BELLA VITA*

Andiamo a mangiare da mamma sta-sera?	Shall we have dinner at mom's tonight?
Devo chiamare i genitori.	I must call my parents.
Possiamo portare i bambini?	Can we bring the kids?
Ci saranno altri ragazzi?	Will there be other kids there?
Questa domenica andiamo a un pranzo di famiglia.	We're going out for lunch with the family on Sunday.
I nonni danno i buoni consigli.	Grandparents give good advice.
Sono fortunato/a di aver un gruppo di amici stretti.	I'm lucky to have a group of close friends.
Vuoi il solito?	Do you want the (your) usual (order)?
Auguri per il tuo onomastico.	Best wishes on your saint's day.
Perché oggi non facciamo un bel picnic?	Why don't we have a nice picnic today?
Ti va di fare una passeggiata?	Do you want to go out for a walk?
Siamo fuori città per il ponte.	We're out of town for the holiday weekend.
Sono in vacanza, non controllerò l'e-mail.	I'm on vacation; I won't be checking e-mail.
Quando sono a casa, mi piace staccare la spina.	I like switching off (from work) when I'm at home.

Buona fortuna e godetevi il vostro amore in tutti i sensi! (Good luck and enjoy your love in all the senses!) *Viva gli Italiani e lunga vita alla bella vita.* (Long live Italians and long live the good life.)

YOUR *PARADISO*

SICILY

The largest and most important city in Sicily is Palermo, a fabulously exotic place with a huge variety of architectural styles providing a stark reminder of its rich and fascinating history as a repeatedly occupied location. One thing you must do here is visit the outdoor markets, in particular the Vucciria, world famous for its luscious produce and stunning, sensual visual displays, captured by the painter Renato Guttuso. If you are keen on archaeological ruins, then Agrigento has one of the finest ancient Greek sites in the world, called the Valley of the Temples. Or you could go to Siracusa to see the Greek Theatre built in the fifth century BC famed for being one of the largest in antiquity. The cosmopolitan resort of Taormina is renowned for its spectacular views over the sea and Mount Etna. For a truly romantic experience, have a cocktail outside the ancient Roman amphitheatre when sun sets for a visual display to set your hearts aflame.

Sicily can also be used as a base to go island hopping, ideal for visiting the smaller isles off its shores such as Lampedusa, Linosa, and Pantelleria. You could also make the time to visit the

Aeolian Isles, dubbed the seven beauties of Sicily, a group of small volcanic islands, the largest being Lipari, and comprising Salina with its fertile green landscapes, Alicudi and Filicudi with their untamed nature, the more classy Panarea, and the delightful Vulcano and Stromboli.

Sicilian food is one of the gastronomic delights of Italy, so make the most of the opportunity to taste the local culinary delicacies made with delicious fresh ingredients, which often have a strong Arabic and African influence. Oranges are plentiful, so indulge in a glass of freshly squeezed *spremuta* (juice) or try a cooling granita ice. Even if you are watching your weight (almost impossible to do in Italy), you must try some Sicilian pastries or desserts, like *cannoli*, sweet tubes filled with ricotta cheese, or the rich *cassata*, which are particular specialties. The perfect accompaniment to any Sicilian meal, whether it be locally caught fish, pasta, or even a plate of couscous is a glass of the excellent wine produced from this region, and for the perfect partner to your sweets, try some of the famous Marsala dessert wine.

SIMPLE GUIDE TO ITALIAN PRONUNCIATION

This is a very basic guide to Italian pronunciation, so you can get your tongue around some of the words and phrases in this book.

VOWELS

Italian vowels are always pronounced very clearly and when they fall together in a word, vowels are always pronounced separately.

LETTER	PRONUNCIATION	ITALIAN EXAMPLE
a	a as in cat, fact, apple	*casa* (house), *amore* (love)
e before single consonant	ay as in day	*mela* (apple), *sera* (evening)
e before double consonant	e as in met	*festa* (party), *bello* (nice)
i	ee as in feet, meet	*vino* (wine), *io* (I), *insetto* (insect)
o before single consonant	o as in blow, soul	*nome* (name), *amore* (love)
o before double consonant	o as in dog, got	*moda* (fashion), *nostro* (ours), *olio* (oil)
u	oo as in moon, swoon, rule	*fungo* (mushroom), *luna* (moon), *uno* (one)

CONSONANTS

Most consonants are pronounced as in English. The two main exceptions, which are the hardest to remember, are C and G.

LETTER	PRONUNCIATION	ITALIAN EXAMPLE
C + a/o/u or + consonant	k as in kick	*casa* (house), *come* (how), *cucina* (kitchen)
C + e/i	ch as in church	*cena* (dinner), *ciao* (hi), *cioccolata* (chocolate)
Ch	cu as in cup	*che* (what), *chiaro* (clear), *chiesa* (church)

LETTER	PRONUNCIATION	ITALIAN EXAMPLE
G + a/o/u	g as in garden	*gatto* (cat), *gonna* (skirt), *gusto* (taste)
G +e/i	j as in job	*gelato* (ice cream), *gioco* (game)
Also note that S can be pronounced two ways:		
S	s as in house	*pasta*, *testa* (head), *festa* (party)
S	z as in zoo	*rosa* (rose), *musica* (music), *tesoro* (darling)

Where you see a consonant is doubled, the sound is held for twice as long, giving extra emphasis on the letter as an audio clue to the fact that it is doubled (for example *mam-ma*). As far as stress is concerned, the general rule of thumb is that Italian words are usually stressed on the next-to-last syllable, for example *cioc-co-LA-ta*. Though there are several cases where the stress is on the last vowel, generally indicated by an accent: *città*, *perché*, *sarà*, etc.

You will notice that some of the phrases in the book have two options, one ending in an *o* and the other in an *a*: for example *bello/a*, *mio/ mia*. This is because all Italian nouns have a gender (masculine or feminine) and the articles must agree with the gender. So basically, if you're referring to a male object, the word generally ends in an *o*, and for a female object it usually ends in an *a* (there are also two sets of plural forms).

And finally, don't forget all Rs should be rolled with abandon (like a Scottish R in Edinburgh or a Spanish R in *señor*). Practice rolling your Rs by vibrating the tip of your tongue just above your teeth, at the front of your mouth.

INDEX

ABOUT THE AUTHORS

Aminda Leigh has been working as a journalist for twenty years. She spent twelve of those years at the BBC in Britain, working in Local and National Radio and on TV. Her *legami con l'Italia* (links with Italy) began in the 1990s when she started to visit Rome on a regular basis, succumbing to the charms of *la Città Eterna* (the Eternal City) and its inhabitants to the point where she decided to take a sabbatical from the BBC in 2001 to try her hand at living in Italy, rather than only experiencing the city as a *turista* (tourist). She never returned to the BBC and is now permanently based in Rome, now running her own agency, AMROS Media Solutions. Her work as a specialist reporter covering the film and television industries has given her a firsthand opportunity to observe how key stars and personalities exhibit their Italian glamour on the world stage at the Cannes, Berlin, Venice, and Rome Film Festivals. Nonetheless, the appreciation of beauty, the seduction of the senses, and the joy of living are fundamental elements in the lives of *all* Italians, even the most humble, ordinary men and women; you see it on the streets every day. In spite of being surrounded by hoards of charming Italian men, Aminda is single.

Pietro Pesce is not quite a *romano* (Roman born-and-bred), but almost. Thanks to a twist of fate, Pietro was born in Washington, D.C., as his parents happened to be stationed in America for work at the time. However, the pull of his *nonni* (grandparents) back in Italy was strong and Pietro's family moved back to Rome when he was just two years old. Since then, he has made his life and career in Italy, establishing himself as a prize-winning photographer, though he is not, as he is keen to stress, one of those infamous *paparazzi*, stealing long-lens pictures of celebrities in compromising or private situations. He first specialized in the heady and complex intrigues of *la politica* (Italian politics), with his work widely published in Italy and also in countries like Spain, the United States, and France. At the beginning of the new millennium, he decided to make a move into the cinema industry. His photo shoot experiences with Italian and international *divi* (divas) have certainly given him a unique perspective on the mysterious nature of style, flair, and "star quality." Pietro and his childhood sweetheart married young and had two children, now teenagers well on their way to becoming full-fledged Italian men. Unfortunately, the marriage ended in divorce, but this hasn't jaded Pietro's passion for love and life, though he has resisted retying the knot just yet.

Getting Where Women Really Belong

- Trying to lose the losers you've been dating?
- Striving to find the time to be a doting mother, dedicated employee, and still be a hot piece of you-know-what in the bedroom?
- Been in a comfortable relationship that's becoming, well, too comfortable?

Don't despair! Visit the Jane on Top blog—your new source for information (and commiseration) on all things relationships, sex, and the juggling act that is being a modern gal.